D1097518

Making the Peace Treaties

1941–1947

*A history of the making of the peace begin-
ning with the Atlantic Charter, the Yalta and
Potsdam Conferences, and culminating in the
drafting of peace treaties with Italy, Bulgaria,
Hungary, Rumania, and Finland*

DEPARTMENT OF STATE   WASHINGTON, D. C.

February 1947

DEPARTMENT OF STATE

Publication 2774

European Series 24

United States Government Printing Office, Washington, D. C.

CONTENTS

III

PAGE

MAPS

LIST a

APPENDIXES

LIST 6

PUBLICATIONS CONTAINING SOURCE MATERIAL

1. *Peace and War: United States Foreign Policy, 1931–1941.* U.S. Government Printing Office, Washington, D.C., 1943. Department of State publication 1983.

2. *Toward the Peace—Documents.* (Texts of major declarations by United Nations, from Atlantic Charter through the Act of Chapultepec.) U.S. Government Printing Office, Washington, D.C., 1945. Department of State publication 2298.

3. "Message of the President to the Congress on the State of the Nation", *Department of State Bulletin,* January 9, 1943, p. 15.

4. *Eleventh Report to Congress on Lend-Lease Operations. For the Period Ended July 31, 1943.* U.S. Government Printing Office, Washington, D.C., 1943.

5. *Charter of the United Nations Together With the Statute of the International Court of Justice, Signed at United Nations Conference on International Organization, San Francisco, California, June 26, 1945.* U.S. Government Printing Office, Washington, D.C., 1945. Department of State publication 2353, Conference Series 74.

6. *United States and Italy, 1936–1946. Documentary Record.* U.S. Government Printing Office, Washington, D.C., 1946. Department of State publication 2669, European Series 17.

7. "Armistice Terms for Rumania", *Department of State Bulletin,* September 17, 1944, p. 289.

8. "Armistice Terms for Bulgaria", *Department of State Bulletin,* October 29, 1944, p. 492; November 19, 1944, p. 616.

9. "Armistice With Finland", *Department of State Bulletin,* February 18, 1945, p. 261.

10. "Armistice Terms for Hungary", *Department of State Bulletin,* January 21, 1945, p. 83.

11. "American Foreign Policy", Address by the President, *Department of State Bulletin,* October 22, 1944, p. 447.

12. *Occupation of Japan, Policy and Progress.* U.S. Government Printing Office, Washington, D.C., 1946. Department of State publication 2671, Far Eastern Series 17.

13. *Report to the Congress of the United States by President Franklin D. Roosevelt, March 1, 1945.* House Document No. 106, 79th Congress, First Session, U.S. Government Printing Office, Washington, 1945, or *Department of State Bulletin,* March 4, 1945, p. 321.

14. "Tripartite Conference at Berlin", *Department of State Bulletin,* August 5, 1945, p. 153.

15. "Restatement of Foreign Policy of the United States", Address by the President, *Department of State Bulletin,* October 28, 1945, p. 653.

16. *Moscow Meeting of Foreign Ministers, December 16–26, 1945. Report by James F. Byrnes, Secretary of State, and Soviet-Anglo-American Communiqué.* U.S. Government Printing Office, Washington, D.C., 1946. Department of State publication 2448, Conference Series 79, or *Department of State Bulletin,* December 30, 1945, p. 1033.

I. First Principles of Peacemaking

» «

A. The Four Freedoms, January 7, 1941, and the Atlantic Charter, August 14, 1941

THE BROAD principles upon which the United States and its Allies sought to make peace after the defeat of the Axis and its satellites were stated by the President of the United States, Franklin Delano Roosevelt, in his message to Congress of January 7, 1941 (b–1)[1]. The President said: "we look forward to a world founded upon four essential human freedoms . . . freedom of speech and expression . . . freedom of every person to worship God in his own way . . . freedom from want . . . freedom from fear".

These principles were elaborated in the Atlantic Charter (b–2) which was issued on August 14, 1941 by President Roosevelt and the Prime Minister of the United Kingdom, Winston Churchill. This document was drafted during meetings between Mr. Roosevelt, Mr. Churchill, and their advisers aboard the British battleship *Prince of Wales* and the U. S. cruiser *Augusta* in the guarded secrecy of Newfoundland's Placentia Bay.

The Atlantic Charter was issued at a time when the Axis was nearly at the peak of its aggressive powers. The Nazis and their allies in Europe had occupied France, Belgium and the Netherlands, Denmark and Norway, Yugoslavia and Greece. They were striking deep into the territory of the Soviet Union. In Africa, they were grouping for a drive on Egypt and the Suez Canal. In the Atlantic, their submarines were taking a heavy toll of cargoes which the United Kingdom and the Soviet Union needed to continue their resistance. In the Far East, Japan had extended its undeclared war far down the coast of China.

The Atlantic Charter established common principles on which the United States and the United Kingdom based their hopes for a better

---

[1] The references labeled "a" and "b" throughout the text indicate List a, which includes the Appendixes contained in this volume, and List b, which is the list of Publications Containing Source Material. Both lists may be found in the Contents.

future for the world. These principles, declared to be inherent in the national policies of the two nations, were:

(1) No material gains out of the war

(2) No territorial changes, except those which are desired by the peoples concerned

(3) All peoples to have the right to choose their own form of government

(4) All peoples who were forcibly deprived of sovereign rights and self-government to have those losses restored

(5) A peace guaranteeing the safety of all nations and enabling the peoples of those nations to be free from fear and want

(6) A wider and permanent system of general security

(7) All nations to have access, on equal terms, to the trade and raw materials of the world

(8) Fullest economic collaboration between all nations toward improved labor standards, economic advancement, and social security.

B. Declaration by United Nations, January 1, 1942

Approximately four months later, on December 7, 1941, Japan attacked Pearl Harbor. By December 11, by congressional declaration, the United States was at war with Japan, Germany, and Italy, all of which first had declared war on the United States.

On January 1, 1942, some five months after the Atlantic Charter was issued, the principles of the Charter were subscribed to by 24 nations in addition to the United States and the United Kingdom in a document called Declaration by United Nations (b–2). These 24 nations were:

The Union of Soviet Socialist Republics, China, Australia, Belgium, Canada, Costa Rica, Cuba, Czechoslovakia, Dominican Republic, El Salvador, Greece, Guatemala, Haiti, Honduras, India, Luxembourg, the Netherlands, New Zealand, Nicaragua, Norway, Panama, Poland, South Africa, and Yugoslavia.

During the course of the war, 19 other nations signed the Declaration. They were:

Mexico, the Philippine Commonwealth, Ethiopia, Iraq, Brazil, Bolivia, Iran, Colombia, Liberia, France, Ecuador, Peru, Chile, Paraguay, Venezuela, Uruguay, Turkey, Egypt, and Saudi Arabia.

These 45 nations declared that "complete victory over their enemies is essential to defend life, liberty, independence and religious freedom, and to preserve human rights and justice in their own lands as well as in other lands, and that they are now engaged in a common struggle against savage and brutal forces seeking to subjugate the world".

Each promised cooperation with the others and that it would not make a separate armistice or peace.

During the next 12 months the military fortunes of the Allies reached their lowest point in the war and then began to rise. In Europe, forces of the Soviet Union drove the Nazis back from Stalingrad. In Africa, forces of the United Kingdom defeated the Nazis at El Alamein, and Anglo-American forces successfully landed in Morocco and Algeria. In the Far East, United States forces established themselves on Guadalcanal.

C. Additional Principles of Peacemaking

During this tide in the war President Roosevelt set forth additional principles of peacemaking. On January 7, 1943 he declared in his Message to Congress on the State of the Nation (b–3) that Germany and Japan must be disarmed and kept disarmed. He said, too, that they must abandon the philosophy of fascism.

A few weeks later—during the conference at Casablanca held between January 14 and January 26, 1943 by the heads of government and staffs of the United States and the United Kingdom—he told a press conference that the United Nations would end the war only on terms of unconditional surrender. He declared, on August 25, 1943, in his letter to Congress transmitting the eleventh report on lend-lease operations (b–4) : "Except for the responsible fascist leaders, the people of the Axis need not fear unconditional surrender to the United Nations. . . . The people of Axis-controlled areas may be assured that when they agree to unconditional surrender they will not be trading Axis despotism for ruin under the United Nations. The goal of the United Nations is to permit liberated peoples to create a free political life of their own choosing and to attain economic security."

The first principles of peacemaking now had been laid. They included :

(1) The points stated in the Atlantic Charter

(2) The stipulations in the Declaration by United Nations that there must be complete victory and that there would be no separate armistice or peace

(3) Disarmament, denazification, unconditional surrender, and no punitive peace for the enemy.

II. Making Peace and Keeping Peace: A Dual Problem

» «

A. First Meeting of the Foreign Secretaries of the United States, United Kingdom, and Soviet Union

A T Moscow, between October 19 and October 30, 1943, the United States, the United Kingdom, and the Soviet Union through their Foreign Secretaries (Cordell Hull, Anthony Eden, and Vyacheslav M. Molotov) reached agreements which implied the realization that the making of peace and the keeping of peace could best be achieved if this work were looked upon not as one problem but as two related problems.

1. Peacekeeping (Declaration of Four Nations)

The Anglo-Soviet-American Communiqué, issued on November 1, 1943 (b–2), declared that there was "unanimous recognition by the three Governments that it was essential in their own national interests and in the interest of all peace-loving nations to continue the present close collaboration and cooperation in the conduct of the war into the period following the end of hostilities, and that only in this way could peace be maintained and the political, economic and social welfare of their peoples fully promoted."

The Declaration of Four Nations on General Security (the U.S., U.K., U.S.S.R., and China), which also was issued on November 1, 1943 (b–2), added that "they recognise the necessity of establishing at the earliest practicable date a general international organization, based on the principle of the sovereign equality of all peace-loving states, and open to membership by all such states, large and small, for the maintenance of international peace and security."

As a result of the Declaration, toward the end of keeping the peace, there were held the Washington Conversations at Dumbarton Oaks on International Peace and Security Organization. These Conversations were held between August 21 and October 7, 1944, among the United States, the United Kingdom, and the Soviet Union on the one hand and, on the other, among the United States, the United Kingdom, and China. In turn, these Conversations were followed by the meeting at San Francisco of 50 countries, between April 25 and June

26, 1945, during which period the Charter of the United Nations (b–5) was drafted.

2. Peacemaking (Declaration Regarding Italy and Declaration on Austria)

The Foreign Secretaries of the United States, the United Kingdom, and the Soviet Union during their meeting in Moscow also reached concrete agreements concerned with making the peace.

In their Declaration Regarding Italy, released on November 1, 1943 (b–2), the Foreign Secretaries stated that "their three Governments are in complete agreement that Allied policy towards Italy must be based upon the fundamental principle that Fascism and all its evil influences and emanations shall be utterly destroyed and that the Italian people shall be given every opportunity to establish governmental and other institutions based upon democratic principles. . . . Freedom of speech, of religious worship, of political belief, of the press and of public meeting shall be restored in full measure to the Italian people . . . ."

In their Declaration on Austria, also released on November 1 (b–2), they stated that "They regard the annexation imposed upon Austria by Germany on March 15th, 1938, as null and void . . . . They declare that they wish to see reestablished a free and independent Austria, and thereby to open the way for the Austrian people themselves, as well as those neighboring states which will be faced with similar problems, to find that political and economic security which is the only basis for lasting peace."

B. The Tehran Conference, November 1943: Confirmation of the Agreements Reached at Moscow

As a consequence of the progress achieved by the Foreign Secretaries at Moscow there was held at Tehran, in November 1943, a meeting of the heads of Government of the United States, the United Kingdom, and the Soviet Union. At Tehran the basic responsibility of the Great Powers in making the peace was reiterated.

The Declaration of the Three Powers, issued on December 1, 1943 (b–2), declared: "We—the President of the United States, the Prime Minister of Great Britain, and the Premier of the Soviet Union, . . . recognize fully the supreme responsibility resting upon us and all the United Nations to make a peace which will command the goodwill of the overwhelming mass of the peoples of the world and banish the scourge and terror of war for many generations."

III.   Surrenders and Armistices

»«

A. *Italy, September 3, 1943*

THE FIRST MEMBER of the Axis to surrender unconditionally was Italy. This event took place on September 3, 1943 as Anglo-American forces crossed over from Sicily and landed on the toe of the Italian Peninsula. An armistice with the United States and the United Kingdom was signed by Marshal Pietro Badoglio who had been appointed Premier by the King of Italy after Benito Mussolini was forced to resign on July 25. The armistice (b–6), a purely military document, provided that "Other conditions of a political, economic and financial nature with which Italy will be bound to comply will be transmitted at a later date."

Within the same month Italy began to move toward a position of military cooperation with the United Nations and against her former Axis allies.

On September 23 a Memorandum of Agreement on the Employment and Disposition of the Italian Fleet and Mercantile Marine (b–6) was signed by the United States, the United Kingdom, and the Italian Government. In this document it was declared that, since the armistice, the King of Italy and the Italian Government had "expressed the wish that the Fleet and the Italian Mercantile Marine should be employed in the Allied effort to assist in the prosecution of the war against the Axis powers . . ."

On September 29 the United States, the United Kingdom, and Italy signed additional conditions to the armistice. In this document, as modified by the protocol signed on November 9 (b–6), it was agreed that Mussolini and others on the United Nations' list of war criminals who could be apprehended by the Italian Government would be handed over to the United Nations. All fascist organizations would be disbanded and de-fascistization fulfilled by the Italian Government. "All Italian laws involving discrimination on grounds of race, color, creed or political opinions" would be rescinded and persons held under such laws given their full release.

Also on September 29 General Eisenhower, Commander in Chief of the Allied armies in Italy, declared in a letter to Marshal Badoglio

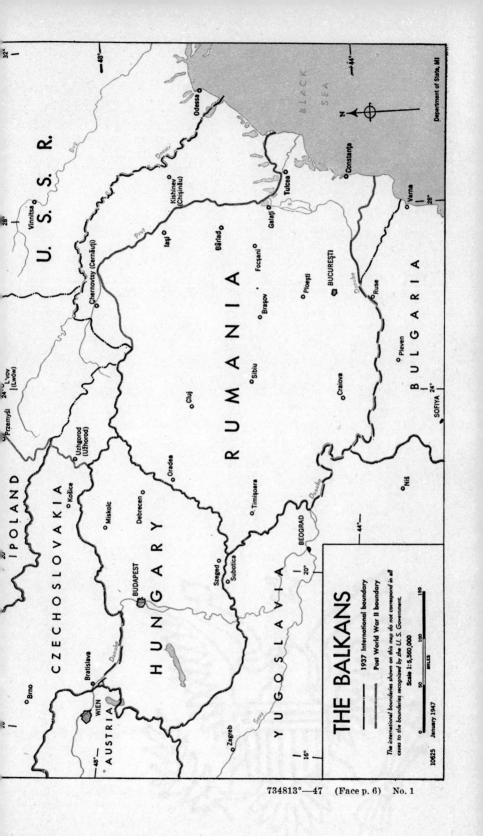

THE BALKANS

—— 1937 International boundary

—— Post World War II boundary

The international boundaries shown on this map do not correspond in all cases to the boundaries recognized by the U. S. Government.

Scale 1:5,560,000

MILES

0   50   100   150

10625   January 1947

Department of State, MI

BLACK SEA

U. S. S. R.

POLAND

CZECHOSLOVAKIA

AUSTRIA

HUNGARY

RUMANIA

YUGOSLAVIA

BULGARIA

Brno

Przemyśl

L'vov (Lwów)

Vinnitsa

Košice

Uzhgorod (Užhorod)

Chernovtsy (Cernăuți)

Kishinev (Chișinău)

Odessa

Bratislava

WIEN

BUDAPEST

Miskolc

Debrecen

Oradea

Cluj

Iași

Bârlad

Galați

Tulcea

Constanța

Szeged

Subotica

Timișoara

BEOGRAD

Sibiu

Brașov

Focșani

Ploești

BUCUREȘTI

Ruse

Varna

Zagreb

Niš

Craiova

Pleven

SOFIYA

Danube

Danube

Sava

Prut

Dnestr

Bug

BLACK SEA

N

FINLAND 1946

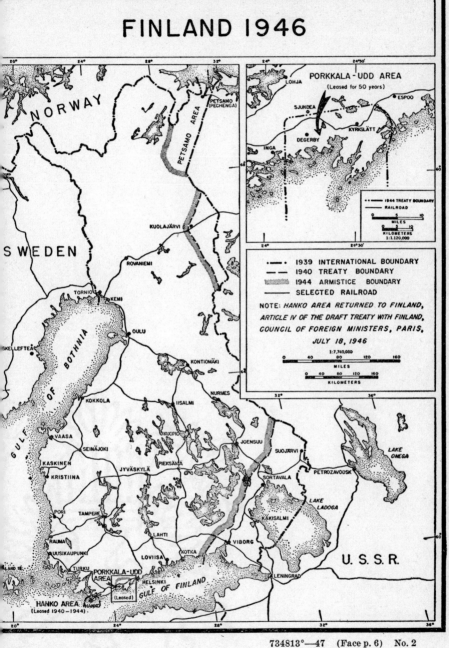

(b–6) that Italy had "become in effect a co-operator with the United Nations."

On October 13, 1943 Italy declared war on and thereby became a co-belligerent in the war against Germany. Italy also declared war on Japan, on July 15, 1945.

B. *Rumania, August 23, 1944*

The second member of the Axis to capitulate was Rumania. This nation accepted the armistice terms of the United States, the United Kingdom, and the Soviet Union on August 23, 1944, declared war on Germany and Hungary on August 24, and signed armistice terms with the United Nations on September 12 (b–7).

The armistice with Rumania contained, in addition to military clauses, the following main provisions:

(1) The Soviet-Rumanian frontier of 1940 would be restored. On the other hand Rumania would regain the area of northern Transylvania which Hitler had taken during the war and given to Hungary.

(2) All persons who had been imprisoned for such reasons as racial origin would be released and legislation upholding such imprisonment or restrictions would be repealed.

(3) The Soviet Union would receive from Rumania, as partial compensation for Rumanian occupation of Soviet territories, three hundred million dollars worth of commodities, payable over six years. Rumania also would make compensation for losses caused to the property of other Allied states and their nationals in Rumania.

(4) Rumania would immediately dissolve and prevent the future existence of all Fascist-type organizations, "whether political, military or para-military, as well as other organizations conducting propaganda hostile to the United Nations, in particular to the Soviet Union . . ."

(5) Rumania would make regular payments in currency and provide the goods and services necessary for the occupation forces.

(6) There would be established an Allied Control Commission, under the chairmanship of the Soviet Union, acting for the Allied powers. This Control Commission would see that the armistice terms were carried out and would function until peace was made with Rumania.

C. *Bulgaria, September 9, 1944*

Bulgaria, which accepted the armistice terms of the Soviet Union on September 9, 1944, signed an armistice with the Soviet Union, the United States, and the United Kingdom on October 28 (b–8). In addition to military clauses, the Bulgarian armistice contained the following main provisions:

(1) Bulgaria would repeal all laws relating to the annexation or incorporation into Bulgaria of Greek or Yugoslav territory.

(2) As in the case of Rumania, Bulgaria would free all persons imprisoned because of racial origin and repeal such discriminatory laws and restrictions.

(3) Bulgaria would cooperate in arresting and trying war criminals.

(4) Bulgaria, again as in the case with Rumania, would wipe out and prevent the future existence of Fascist-type organizations.

(5) Bulgarian reparation to the United Nations would be determined later.

(6) Bulgaria would make regular payments in currency and provide the goods and services necessary for the occupation forces.

(7) Until a peace treaty was signed with Bulgaria, an Allied Control Commission would regulate and supervise the execution of the armistice terms. This Control Commission would be under the chairmanship of the Soviet Union, but there would be participation by representatives of the United States and the United Kingdom.

D. *Finland, September 19, 1944*

Finland signed the armistice terms of the Soviet Union and the United Kingdom (the United States was not at war with Finland) on September 19, 1944 (b–9). On March 3, 1945 the Finnish Prime Minister declared that Finland had been at war with Germany since September 15, 1944. In addition to the military clauses, the armistice with Finland restored the terms of the treaty of 1940 between the Soviet Union and Finland, except for changes stipulated in the armistice.

Petsamo, the important warm-water port on the Barents Sea, was ceded to the Soviet Union. The Soviet Union relinquished its right to the lease on the Peninsula of Hangö in the Baltic. However, the Soviet Union was given the right to establish a naval base in the area of Porkkala-Udd, which controlled the approaches to Leningrad. The Soviet Union would get from Finland, as compensation for damage to and occupation of Soviet territories, three hundred million dollars worth of commodities, payable over six years. Future provision would be made for compensation to other Allied states and their nationals for losses of property in Finland during the war.

The armistice with Finland established—as in the armistices with Rumania and Bulgaria—that Finland would cooperate in arresting and judging war criminals; in freeing persons arrested because of their racial origin and in repealing such laws; and in dissolving Fascist-type organizations. Similarly, the armistice provided for an Allied Control Commission, under the chairmanship of the Soviet Union, acting on behalf of the Allied powers.

E. Hungary, January 20, 1945

Hungary, the last remaining fighting satellite of the Axis in Europe, capitulated four months later. On January 20, 1945 it signed an armistice with the United States, the United Kingdom, and the Soviet Union (b–10). In addition to military clauses, there were provisions in the armistice which established that Hungary would:

(1) Withdraw from territories of Czechoslovakia, Yugoslavia, and Rumania and repeal all legislation relating to annexation or incorporation of such territories.

(2) Put into effect stringent and far-reaching provisions for the protection of those persons in Hungary who had religious beliefs and origins different from the majority of Hungarians.

(3) Make reparation to the Soviet Union, Czechoslovakia, and Yugoslavia to the amount of three hundred million dollars' worth of commodities, payable over six years. Of this amount the Soviet Union would get two hundred millions.

(4) Compensate other Allied states and their nationals for property losses suffered in Hungary during the war.

(5) Wipe out Fascist-type organizations.

(6) Make regular payments in currency and provide the goods and services necessary for the occupation forces.

The Hungarian armistice also provided for the establishment in Hungary of an Allied Control Commission, under the chairmanship of the Soviet Union, with the participation of representatives of the United States and the United Kingdom.

IV.   Peacemaking at Yalta and at Potsdam

» «

A. The Yalta Conference, February 3–11, 1945

IN THE PERIOD between the meetings at Tehran and Yalta, Anglo-American forces landed in Normandy: they liberated France, Belgium, and part of the Netherlands; took Aachen in Germany; defeated the Nazi thrust in the Ardennes; and prepared an offensive across the Roer River into Germany. Soviet forces captured Warsaw and penetrated Germany from the east.

As victory approached, President Roosevelt reiterated certain basic peacemaking principles and emphasized new ones. In his speech before the Foreign Policy Association, on October 21, 1944 (b–11), he stressed again that the Allies did not seek to achieve a punitive peace and that the enemy would be disarmed. He said that war criminals would be punished. He emphasized that the cooperation of the Big Powers in the making of peace was a vital necessity. If they did not continue to work together, they some day might have to fight each other.

In connection with this latter point the President declared in his Message to Congress of January 6, 1945 (b–2) that:

(1) There were differences among the nations.

(2) Mistakes and disappointments were inevitable in peacemaking.

(3) The American people must be watchful not to exploit and exaggerate the differences between the United States and its Allies.

The next month, between February 3 and February 11, the heads of government of the United States, the United Kingdom, and the Soviet Union, and the Foreign Secretaries of the three powers met at Yalta, in the Crimea section of the Soviet Union. Many wide-ranging agreements were reached. They were recorded in a joint report, issued on February 11, 1945 (b–2), and in an Agreement Regarding Japan, which was not made public until February 11, 1946 (b–12). (At the time of the Yalta conference the Soviet Union was not at war with Japan and publication of the Agreement at that time might have caused a disruption of the Allies' military strategy.)

1. Territorial Changes

The three powers' territorial agreements concerning Europe chiefly affected Poland, the Soviet Union, and Germany. Poland's eastern boundary would become the Curzon line which, drawn in 1919, lay west of Poland's 1937 boundary with the Soviet Union. For this loss of territory Poland would be compensated in the west at Germany's expense. Other territorial agreements involved the Far East.

2. Political Agreements

The terms of unconditional surrender were reiterated.

Specific plans were laid down for the occupation and control of Germany; if France desired, she could participate.

Germany would be disarmed and denazified.

Germany would not be the subject of a punitive peace.

"Democratic means" would be employed to assist Europe's liberated peoples. The three powers would act jointly to help the liberated peoples create democratic institutions of their own choice.

It also was decided by the three powers that discussions among their Foreign Secretaries were of great value and that they should be held as often as possible, probably every three or four months.

The three powers further agreed that "Only with the continuing and growing cooperation and understanding among our three countries and among all the peace-loving nations can the highest aspiration of humanity be realized—a secure and lasting peace which will, in the words of the Atlantic Charter, 'afford assurance that all the men in all the lands may live out their lives in freedom from fear and want.' "

3. Report to the American People

President Roosevelt reported to the American people on March 1 on the peacemaking at Yalta. In a speech before a joint session of the Senate and the House of Representatives (b–13), he declared that the Yalta conference "was a successful effort by the three leading nations to find a common ground for peace. It spells the end of the system of unilateral action and exclusive alliances and spheres of influence and balances of power and all the other expedients which have been tried for centuries—and have failed."

But, the President emphasized: ". . . unless you here in the halls of the American Congress—with the support of the American people—concur in the decisions reached at Yalta, and give them your active support, the meeting will not have produced lasting results."

B. *The Potsdam Conference, July 17–August 2, 1945*

Within the six-month period that separated the meetings at Yalta and Potsdam, President Roosevelt died on April 12; the surrender of Germany was announced and formally ratified by the United States, the United Kingdom, the Soviet Union, and France on May 8; the Japanese Empire was battered to the status of a besieged island fortress.

At the Potsdam Conference, held between July 17 and August 2, 1945, the President of the United States was Harry S. Truman and the Secretary of State was James F. Byrnes. Until midway in the Conference when election returns were totaled, the Prime Minister of the United Kingdom was Winston Churchill. Following the elections he was replaced by Clement Attlee, and Anthony Eden was replaced as Foreign Minister by Ernest Bevin. The Soviet Union's representatives were Generalissimo Stalin and Vyacheslav M. Molotov.

Peacemaking decisions concerned the Far East as well as Europe. The agreements relating to Japan (to which the Soviet Union was not a party, since it was not then at war with Japan) were issued on July 26, by the United States, the United Kingdom, and China, as a Proclamation Defining Terms for Japanese Surrender (b–12). The Proclamation stated the basic principles of peacemaking which already had been laid down.

Most of the peacemaking agreements of the United States, the United Kingdom, and the Soviet Union for Europe were set down in the report on the Tripartite Conference at Berlin, which was released on August 2 (b–14).

This tripartite report dealt with the occupation of Germany, reparation from Germany, the boundaries of Germany, and the future of Germany. It confirmed the decision reached at Yalta that Germany should be divided into zones of occupation for purposes of military government.

1. Occupation of Germany

The following common political aims were stated in the tripartite report. (1) "So far as is practicable, there shall be uniformity of treatment of the German population throughout Germany." (2) "The administration of affairs in Germany should be directed towards the decentralization of the political structure and the development of local responsibility." (3) "For the time being no central German government shall be established."

Common economic goals also were established. (1) "At the earliest practicable date, the German economy shall be decentralized for the purpose of eliminating the present excessive concentration of economic power as exemplified in particular by cartels, syndicates, trusts and other monopolistic arrangements." (2) "In organizing the German economy, primary emphasis shall be given to the development of agriculture and peaceful domestic industries." (3) "During the period of occupation Germany shall be treated as a single economic unit."

2. Reparation From Germany

It also was agreed that Germany should be compelled to compensate to the greatest possible extent for the loss and suffering caused the United Nations. Reparation claims were to be met by removals of industrial plant and equipment and from appropriate German external assets. However, sufficient resources were to be left to Germany to enable the German people to have a standard of living which would not be higher than the average in Europe, excluding the United Kingdom and the Soviet Union. (The determination of reparation shares for Allied claimants other than the Soviet Union and Poland was made later at the Paris Conference on Reparation which was held in the fall of 1945.)

3. The Boundaries of Germany

Germany would lose territory.

The President of the United States and the British Prime Minister agreed to support at a forthcoming peace settlement "the proposal of the Soviet Government concerning the ultimate transfer to the Soviet Union of the City of Koenigsberg and the area adjacent to it . . ."

In regard to Poland a more limited yet equally clear agreement was reached among the three powers. Poland was to administer Upper and Lower Silesia and parts of East Prussia, Brandenburg, and Pomerania, "pending the final determination of Poland's western frontier," which would be drawn in the peace treaty for Germany.

4. The Future of Germany

The tripartite report also declared that "It is the intention of the Allies that the German people be given the opportunity to prepare for the eventual reconstruction of their life on a democratic and peaceful basis. If their own efforts are steadily directed to this end, it will be possible for them in due course to take their place among the free and peaceful peoples of the world."

5. The Council of Foreign Ministers

The tripartite report also detailed the "establishment of a Council of Foreign Ministers representing the five principal powers" (the U.S., U.S.S.R., U.K., France, and China).

The Council's "immediate important task" was "to draw up, with a view to their submission to the United Nations, treaties of peace with Italy, Rumania, Bulgaria, Hungary and Finland, and to propose settlements of territorial questions outstanding on the termination of the war in Europe."

The Council also would prepare "a peace settlement for Germany to be accepted by the government of Germany when a government adequate for the purpose is established."

The Council's peacemaking activities would start with Italy and these four Axis satellites instead of with Germany because, as Secretary Byrnes explained, during a broadcast on July 15, 1946 (a–6) :

"It was obvious then (during the Potsdam Conference) that the making of peace with Germany would take time. There was no German government to deal with, and no agreement as to how soon we should permit a German government to function. It was equally obvious that a start could be made toward making peace with Italy and the states which were satellites of the Axis. They had governments. So we started there."

Not all the five powers represented in the Council of Foreign Ministers would be party to the drafting of each of these five treaties. As each of these treaties was drafted, the Council would be "composed of the members representing those states which were signatory to the terms of surrender imposed upon the enemy state concerned. For the purpose of the peace settlement for Italy," declared the three powers, "France shall be regarded as a signatory to the terms of surrender for Italy." (b–14).

The Council of Foreign Ministers would be in continuous session. When the Foreign Ministers themselves were not present their work would be carried on by "high-ranking" deputies and staffs of "technical advisers". The permanent seat of the Council's joint secretariat would be London. The Council would hold its first meeting "in London not later than September 1, 1945." Meetings might be held by common agreement in other capitals from time to time.

The Council would not be a substitute for regular meetings of the Foreign Secretaries of the three powers. As agreed at Yalta, there still would be "periodic consultation among the foreign secretaries of the United States, the Union of Soviet Socialist Republics and the United Kingdom."

6. The Waterways of Europe

In a report to the American people on Potsdam, on August 9 (a–1), one week after the Conference ended, President Truman emphasized a problem on which the three powers had not yet reached agreement. This problem concerned regulation of traffic on the waterways of Europe—the Danube River, the Dardanelles and the entire Black Sea straits, the Rhine, the Kiel Canal, and all the inland waterways which border two or more European nations.

The United States wanted navigation on those European waterways to be free and unrestricted, under regulations established by international authorities which would include the United States, the United Kingdom, the Soviet Union, France, and all those states which bordered on the waterways.

In connection with this question, President Truman pointed out: "One of the persistent causes for wars in Europe in the last two centuries has been the selfish control of the waterways of Europe." The fulfilment of the principles of the American proposals, he said, were "important to the future peace and security of the world."

V. First Meeting of the Council of Foreign Ministers in London

» «

FROM SEPTEMBER 11 to October 2, 1945, the Council of Foreign Ministers met in London to discuss the peace treaties with Italy, Rumania, Bulgaria, Hungary, and Finland. Since the Potsdam Conference, two atomic bombs had been dropped on Japan; the Soviet Union, as agreed at Yalta, had declared war on Japan; and the United States, on behalf of the Allies, had accepted Japan's offer to surrender unconditionally.

The major participants at the Council's session in London were Secretary Byrnes of the United States, Foreign Minister Bevin of the United Kingdom, and Foreign Minister Molotov of the Soviet Union.

A. Agreement on Human Rights

The Council made important peacemaking decisions. One was that the treaties with Italy, Rumania, Bulgaria, Hungary, and Finland should include a bill of rights under which these five defeated nations would guarantee their citizens freedom of speech, religious worship, political belief, and public meeting. This decision fulfilled an agreement reached by the Foreign Secretaries of the United States, the United Kingdom, and the Soviet Union during their meeting in Moscow in 1943 (b–2). It also confirmed the human rights and fundamental freedoms set forth in the Charter of the United Nations.

B. Agreements Connected With the Italian Treaty

Most of the Council's work concerned the treaty with Italy, aside from Germany and Japan the biggest peacemaking problem. It was agreed that:

(*a*) On the conclusion of the treaty Italian sovereignty would be restored. This would permit withdrawal of foreign troops and, except as specified in the treaty, termination of foreign controls within Italy.

(*b*) The Dodecanese Islands, strategically placed in relation to the Suez Canal and the Dardanelles, were to be ceded to Greece, which had an historic claim to the islands and their population of 150,000 Greeks.

(Final agreement on this matter awaited only the assent of the Soviet Union, which wanted to study "certain questions".)

(c) Italy would lose her colonies in Africa (Libya, Eritrea, and Italian Somaliland). They would come under the trusteeship provisions of the United Nations Charter. The Council would decide the form of trusteeship at a later date.

(d) In connection with the question of boundary adjustments between Italy and Yugoslavia, in the main the new frontier should be governed by "ethnic considerations". Also, within the area of Trieste there would be established a free port under international control.

(e) Italy should rely on the United Nations for protection and devote its resources to the needs of its civilian economy instead of engaging in competition in armaments.

C. *Proposal for an International Conference on the Treaties With Italy, the Three Balkan Nations, and Finland*

One of the major questions which was discussed and not resolved during the session in London was whether a conference of many nations should be called by the Council. The United States, which proposed that it be called, felt that a conference was necessary in order to permit the peacemaking participation of other nations which would be vitally concerned in maintaining and enforcing the peace settlements for Italy, the Balkan nations, and Finland, on which the Council was working.

In connection with this issue Secretary Byrnes said, on October 5, in a report he made to the American people (a–2) : "none of us can expect to write the peace in our own way. If this hard reality is accepted by statesmen and peoples at an early stage of the peacemaking process, it may at later stages save us and save the peace of the world from the disastrous effects of disillusionment and intransigences."

D. *The Question of Reparation From Italy*

Another unresolved question concerned reparation from Italy. The Soviet Union thought that Italian reparation should amount to three hundred million dollars' worth of commodities, of which the Soviet Union would get one hundred million and Greece, Yugoslavia, and Albania two hundred million. The United States, which was asking for no reparation, considered that this was more reparation than the Italian economy could provide.

E. The Attitude of the United States

In his report on the London session of the Council, Secretary Byrnes declared that he had hopes for greater peacemaking progress in the future. But he said those hopes depended upon the member nations' showing a spirit of intelligent compromise. Without that, declared the Secretary, additional progress was impossible. Unanimous consent, he pointed out, was necessary for agreement in the Council.

At the same time the Secretary defended the Council as an institution. He said that it was best for all nations that the Council perform the primary tasks of peacemaking.

"Experience," said the Secretary, "reveals that a certain degree of understanding among the major powers is essential to secure general agreement among many nations."

Two weeks later, on October 20, President Truman commented in a statement to the Foreign Policy Association that the American people's full participation in solving the problems of peace demands great patience of all and an increasingly clear understanding of the problems of other peoples.

On Navy Day, October 27, the President also told the American people that firmness as well as forbearance was necessary to solve differences among the big powers now "passing through a difficult phase of international relations" (b–15). He emphasized that "differences of the kind that exist today among the nations that fought together so long and so valiantly for victory are not hopeless or irreconcilable. There are no conflicts of interest among the victorious powers so deeply rooted that they can not be resolved. . . . It will require a steadfast adherence to the high principles we have enunciated. It will also require a willingness to find a common ground as to the methods of applying these principles."

VI. The Foreign Ministers of the Big Three, December 16–26, 1945

» «

DURING THE AUTUMN of 1945 the United States sought another meeting of the Foreign Ministers. This was held between December 16 and December 26 in Moscow, by the Foreign Ministers of the United States, United Kingdom, and Soviet Union, in fulfilment of the Yalta understanding that such meetings would be held regularly.

A. Agreement on the Conference at Paris, and for Withdrawal of Troops of Occupation, and Concerning the Stages of Peacemaking

During this meeting, the Foreign Ministers reached agreement concerning a conference of nations to be called in connection with the conclusion of the peace settlements with Italy, Rumania, Bulgaria, Hungary, and Finland (b–16). They suggested, and France later agreed, that the conference should be held in Paris. It would begin no later than May 1, 1946.

These would be the stages of peacemaking, the Foreign Ministers decided at Moscow:

(*a*) The preliminary terms of peace with those five defeated nations would be drawn by members of the Council of Foreign Ministers, as the principal powers which signed the respective armistices.

(*b*) As soon as the preliminary terms were drawn they would be submitted to a conference called by the United States, the United Kingdom, the Soviet Union, France, and China (the Council of Foreign Ministers and the permanent members of the Security Council of the United Nations). This conference would be composed of all those states which had actively waged war with substantial force against the European members of the Axis.

(*c*) During the conference a hearing would be given to representatives of Italy, Rumania, Bulgaria, Hungary, and Finland. Each would be permitted to discuss and present his views on the peace settlement with his nation.

(*d*) The conference would consider the draft treaties prepared by the Council and draw up its recommendations for those treaties.

(*e*) The Council would reconsider the treaties in the light of the recommendations of the conference, and would prepare the final texts of the peace settlements with Italy, Rumania, Bulgaria, Hungary, and Finland.

(*f*) The final texts of these five treaties would be signed by all the states which had actively waged war with those nations.

It also was agreed by the Foreign Ministers that the signing of the peace treaties with Italy, the three Balkan nations, and Finland would make it possible to withdraw from these countries forces of occupation, excepting some troops of the Soviet Union in Rumania and Hungary, through which the Soviet Union maintained its lines of communication with its occupation forces in Austria. This step was vital to world-wide economic recovery, declared Secretary Byrnes on December 30 in the report he made on the Moscow meeting to the American people (a-3).

Other agreements reached during this session at Moscow concerned Allied occupation policy for Japan, and representative governments in Rumania and Bulgaria.

B. *Patience and Firmness, March 16, 1946*

Early in 1946 there was mounting international uneasiness. One reason was the situation in Iran, where Soviet troops were stationed against the wishes of the Iranian Government. On February 28 Secretary Byrnes delivered a speech before the Overseas Press Club in New York City (b-17), which, in effect, was an appeal to reason.

He noted that throughout the world there was suspicion and distrust and that while some suspicions were unfounded, others might not be.

Pointing out that the United States had "openly, gladly, and wholeheartedly welcomed" the Soviet Union as an ally and a "great power, second to none in the family of the United Nations", Mr. Byrnes added that "We have approved many adjustments in her favor and, in the process, resolved many serious doubts in her favor." But the Secretary also said in this connection:

"We have no right to hold our troops in the territories of other sovereign states without their approval and consent freely given.

"We must not unduly prolong the making of peace and continue to impose our troops upon small and impoverished states.

"No power has a right to help itself to alleged enemy properties in liberated or ex-satellite countries before a reparation settlement has been agreed upon by the Allies. We have not and will not agree to any one power deciding for itself what it will take from these countries.

"We must not conduct a war of nerves to achieve strategic ends.

"We do not want to stumble and stagger into situations where no power intends war but no power will be able to avert war."

Approximately two weeks later, on March 16, Secretary Byrnes, in a speech before the Society of the Friendly Sons of St. Patrick in New York City (b–18), emphasized the need to maintain within the civilian traditions of the United States "our military strength at a level to match our responsibilities in the world." He said, too:

"It takes time to pass from the psychology of war to the psychology of peace. We must have patience, as well as firmness. We must keep our feet on the ground. We cannot afford to lose our tempers. . . . we must and shall achieve a just and enduring peace for ourselves and all nations."

On Army Day, April 6, President Truman told the American people that as a consequence of the strength of the United States, "we have to assume leadership and accept responsibility" in the peacemaking.

VII. The Council of Foreign Ministers in Paris, April 25-May 16, 1946

» «

THE SECOND SESSION of the Council of Foreign Ministers began, in Paris, on April 25, 1946. This meeting took place in consequence of a request, on April 4, from Secretary Byrnes to Foreign Ministers Bevin, Molotov, and Bidault. The Secretary indicated that time was running out on the agreement of the Foreign Ministers at Moscow that the Council's draft treaties for Italy, the three Balkan nations, and Finland should be prepared and presented to a conference of nations no later than May 1.

As the Council session got under way in Paris the major participants were Messrs. Byrnes, Bevin, Molotov, and Bidault. Two of Mr. Byrnes' closest and most important advisers at this and all other subsequent international conferences in which he participated were Senator Tom Connally, of Texas, then chairman of the Foreign Relations Committee of the Senate, and Senator Arthur H. Vandenberg, of Michigan, a member of and later chairman of this committee.

Of great assistance to these discussions of the Foreign Ministers and their advisers was the work on the treaties with Italy, the three Balkan nations, and Finland which had been done since the London session by the Council's deputies, who had been and would be in continuous session.

In the period between the Council's session in London and its session in Paris the deputies had sent to Trieste a special commission of inquiry to make recommendations on the boundaries between Italy and Yugoslavia. On the basis of recommendations of the French member of the special commission, the Council reached subsequent agreement in regard to Yugoslavia's western frontier. As a result of other work done by the deputies, the foundations were laid for the Council's later agreement on the limitations on the armed forces of Italy, the three Balkan nations, and Finland as specified in the treaties with those five nations.

A. Reparation From Italy

At the Council's session in Paris, the Soviet Union continued to request reparation from Italy amounting to one hundred million dollars' worth of commodities. The United States and the United Kingdom argued against such reparation. The United States still contended that it was not going to advance more millions of dollars to Italy to enable that country to produce goods to be paid as reparation to Allies of the United States.

B. Trusteeship for the Italian Colonies

Within the framework of the Council's agreement at London that the Italian colonies should go under trusteeship, the Soviet Union supported a French proposal that Italy be made trustee for the African colonies. The United Kingdom opposed Italian trusteeship and proposed British trusteeship for Cyrenaica, "for security reasons." The United States believed that the colonies should be placed under United Nations trusteeship. The objective of this trusteeship, said Secretary Byrnes, would be "the welfare of the inhabitants and their independence at the earliest practicable date."

C. The Italo-Yugoslav Border

With regard to the Italo-Yugoslav border the Soviet Union still contended that Venezia Giulia should be treated as an inseparable whole, and that so treated the claim of Yugoslavia to the area was superior to that of Italy. The United States, the United Kingdom, and France believed that a statesmanlike solution was a boundary line which would in the main be an ethnic line, leaving a minimum of people under alien rule. This had been a decision of the Council during its session in London.

D. Treaty Clauses Pertaining to General Commercial Relations and the Problem of the Danube

Among the economic issues discussed was the question of clauses to be inserted in the treaties with Italy, the three Balkan nations, and Finland pertaining to the general commercial relations of these five defeated nations. The United States proposed—but the Council could not agree—that these five defeated countries should grant to the members of the United Nations equality of treatment in commercial relations, pending the conclusion of commercial treaties or agreements.

The Council also discussed and failed to reach agreement on the suggestion of the United States and the United Kingdom that there be incorporated in the treaties with Rumania, Bulgaria, and Hungary a provision concerning freedom of navigation on the Danube River, which Secretary Byrnes called "the gateway to Central Europe," which President Truman had discussed in his report on the Potsdam Conference.

E. *Austria*

In this series of meetings Mr. Byrnes also raised the question of a treaty of peace with Austria. "The making of peace with Austria," Secretary Byrnes pointed out, on May 20, in his subsequent report to the American people (a–4), "is essential to the restoration of anything like conditions of peace in Europe. As long as there is no peace with Austria and foreign troops remain on her soil, military communication lines will continue to be maintained in Rumania and Hungary and possibly Italy", continuing the imposition of unjustified economic and social difficulties upon the peoples of those countries. "If peace could be made with Austria concurrently with the treaties now under consideration", said the Secretary, "there would be no necessity or excuse for a single soldier on foreign soil in Europe with the exception of Germany and a line of communication through Poland."

As justification for consideration by the Council of a peace treaty with Austria, Secretary Byrnes pointed out that the United States, the United Kingdom, and the Soviet Union previously had agreed that Austria should be considered a liberated country. However, no agreement was reached to take up the Austrian treaty at this time.

F. *Germany*

Still another major problem which was brought up by Secretary Byrnes during the first part of the Council's session in Paris was the question of a treaty with Germany, the hub of the entire European peacemaking problem.

Since it had been accepted by the Council that the treaties with Italy, Rumania, Bulgaria, Hungary, and Finland were only a preliminary to a peace treaty with Germany, Secretary Byrnes proposed that the Council appoint immediately "special deputies to prepare a peace settlement (with Germany) which could be considered at a general Allied conference, the date of which should be fixed by the Council". These special deputies also would have the job of reporting on "several pressing problems (in relation to Germany), including boundary and economic questions."

The United States, Mr. Byrnes said, could not continue to carry out the program of reparations removals from the American zone in Germany to the Soviet Union if Germany was not to be administered as an economic unit as agreed upon at Potsdam. Furthermore, declared Mr. Byrnes, "Whatever boundaries are agreed upon for Germany, she must be able to subsist without external assistance. We cannot subsidize Germany to enable her to pay reparations to other nations."

The Council took no action on this proposal of the United States. The Soviet Union told the Council—whose decisions were reached according to the rule of unanimity—that it needed more time to study the proposal.

The United States also proposed, in regard to Germany, that the United Kingdom, Soviet Union, and France, with the United States, sign a treaty guaranteeing the disarmament and demilitarization of Germany for at least 25 years. As a part of this proposal to expand the agreements reached at Potsdam, the United States offered the three other powers, for their consideration, a draft treaty (b–19).

The United States proposed this pact and offered the draft treaty, said Secretary Byrnes, because some nations were making unilateral attempts at achieving "security", which attempts "are said to originate in the fear of the revival of German military might." The Secretary also said "Security is the concern of every nation. But the effort of one nation to increase its security may threaten the security of other nations and cause them in turn to try to increase their own security. The quest for security may lead to less rather than more security in the world."

Both the United Kingdom and France declared that they favored, in principle, the draft treaty offered by the United States. The Soviet Union held that existing agreements for the disarmament and demilitarization of Germany had not been carried out and, until they had been, it would be premature to consider a long-term arrangement as the United States proposed.

G. *Recess of the Paris Meeting of the Council*

After 19 days of virtually inconclusive discussion on the major aspects of the proposed treaties, Secretary Byrnes, on May 14, asked for and was granted a recess of the Council meeting (a–6). In his statement of request, the Secretary declared: ". . . it is likely to facilitate our work if the present session of the Council recesses until June 15, permitting each of us to give undivided attention to reexamination of our positions in the hope of finding means of reconciling them. Such use of our time is calculated to be more fruitful than to extend our present session."

H. Reports of Secretary Byrnes and Senator Vandenberg on the First Part of the Paris Session

During the recess the Secretary, on May 20, reported to the American people (a–4). He discussed the Council's difficulties and disagreements. He pointed out that what the nations were seeking was a "people's peace", and that such a peace had to be hammered out, slowly and doggedly.

Lasting peace could not be achieved through "flashing diplomatic triumphs." It could only be achieved through "patience and firmness, tolerance and understanding."

The Secretary assured the American people: "Our problems are serious, but I am not discouraged. Our offensive to secure peace has only begun. . . . The objective is peace—not a peace founded upon vengeance or greed, but a just peace, the only peace that can endure."

On the following day a report was made on the Paris session by Senator Vandenberg (a–5), one of the two congressional advisers on whom Secretary Byrnes leaned heavily for advice. Senator Vandenberg, fully substantiating the position taken by the Secretary, declared:

"the Council was not a success in gaining agreement upon several key questions upon which the solution of our major problems hangs. It did not achieve agreement on a number of controlling points. It is advisable to be entirely frank upon this score."

But, with Secretary Byrnes, Senator Vandenberg was not discouraged. He emphasized the important role that the United States could and must play in the making of peace. In this connection he stressed the importance of the bipartisan foreign policy of the United States. "I do not despair of the results" of the peacemaking efforts, said the Senator, "particularly if the unselfish voice of America is a united one."

VIII. Second Half of the Council's Session in Paris, June 15–July 12, 1946

» «

ON JUNE 15, 1946, as the Council had agreed, the Foreign Ministers resumed their meetings in Paris, in order that the draft treaties with Italy, the three Balkan nations, and Finland might be completed and the Paris Conference might be called. Once again, at the request of Secretary Byrnes, Senators Connally and Vandenberg were on hand to advise him.

In contrast with the meetings before the recess, the Council was able, by July 12, when it concluded its session, to reach sufficient agreement on the draft treaties to justify the calling of the Paris Conference on July 29.

A. Agreements on the Italo-Yugoslav Boundary and for the Free Territory of Trieste

One of the major decisions reached concerned the Italo-Yugoslav boundary. This established the principle of a Free Territory of Trieste.

After determining that the frontier line proposed by the French member of the Trieste commission represented the greatest measure of agreement possible on a frontier which, in the main, would be an ethnic line, the Council then agreed that Trieste and the adjacent territory along the western coast of the Istrian Peninsula, peopled largely by Italians, would be ceded by Italy but not to Yugoslavia. A Free Territory of Trieste would be constituted, the integrity and independence of which would be assured by the United Nations.

None of the Foreign Ministers considered ideal this agreement establishing the Free Territory of Trieste. But Secretary Byrnes said that it seemed the most reasonable decision which could be reached.

B. Agreements on the Dodecanese Islands and on the Italian Colonies

The problem of the Dodecanese Islands finally was settled. All the members of the Council at last agreed that these strategic Mediterranean islands should go to Greece, with the proviso that they should be, and should remain, demilitarized.

The decision on the trusteeship of the Italian colonies in Africa would be deferred for one year. If at the end of that time the Council did not agree on the ultimate disposition of the colonies, said Secretary Byrnes, "in light of the wishes and welfare of the inhabitants and world peace and security", it was agreed that the Council should turn the problem over to the General Assembly of the United Nations and abide by the decision recommended by that organization.

C. *Agreement on Italian Reparation*

The decision on Italian reparation to the Soviet Union provided that:

(1) The Soviet Union should receive over a seven-year period a total of $100,000,000 payable in commodities and other assets, as recompense for devastation of its territories by Italian armies;

(2) Sources from which reparation payments should be drawn would be limited to specialized machinery of war plants, Italian-owned assets in the satellite countries, and current production; and

(3) The Council powers' four ambassadors at Rome should value the Italian assets transferred to the Soviet Union.

Additional conditions were placed on reparation deliveries out of current production, namely: (*a*) such deliveries should not be required during the first two years, and thereafter should be arranged to avoid interference with Italian economic reconstruction; (*b*) amounts, types, and schedules of production for reparations should be freely negotiated by the two Governments concerned; (*c*) the Soviet Union would supply on commercial terms the required materials normally imported by Italy and needed to produce reparation goods for the Soviet Union; and (*d*) the commercial cost of such materials supplied by the Soviet Union would be deducted from the value of the finished reparation goods.

D. *Austria and Germany*

After the Council had reached the necessary stage of agreement on the five draft treaties, some time again was devoted to Austria and Germany, the crux of Europe's peacemaking problem.

The United States and the United Kingdom offered to the other powers proposed treaty drafts which recognized the independence of Austria and provided for the withdrawal of occupying troops. The United States proposed that, on the basis of these drafts, the deputies of the Foreign Ministers be directed to prepare a peace settlement with Austria.

The Soviet Union proposed, instead, that further action should be taken to insure the denazification of Austria and the removal from

Austria of large numbers of displaced persons who were considered to be unfriendly to the Soviet Union.

The United States, the United Kingdom, and France then proposed that, at one and the same time, the Foreign Ministers' deputies should consider a treaty with Austria, and the Allied Control Council in Germany should investigate and report on the progress of denazification and the problem of displaced persons in Austria. But the Soviet Union felt that more tangible action should be taken on the problems of denazification and displaced persons. Only then could it agree to the deputies' taking up the Austrian treaty.

During the discussions on Germany the Soviet Union still felt that it would be premature for the four powers to consider a treaty to guarantee the demilitarization and disarmament of Germany for at least a generation. Nor was the United States successful in its proposal that the three other powers, each of which also administered a zone in Germany, agree on economic unification of all four zones which originally had been agreed upon at the Potsdam Conference.

The United States then offered to administer its zone in Germany in conjunction with any one or more of the other zones as a single economic unit. Whatever arrangements were made with one government would be open on equal terms to the governments of the other zones at any time that they were prepared to participate. The United Kingdom said it would consider the proposal and indicated a favorable reply would be forthcoming.

E. "Justice, Charity, and Mercy"

With an agreement that the next steps in the peacemaking would be taken at the Paris Conference, which would begin on July 29, the Council ended its session in Paris on July 12.

Secretary Byrnes on July 15 (a–7) and Senator Vandenberg on July 16 (b–20) once again reported to the American people. The Paris Conference, which would consider the five draft treaties, would be no rubber stamp for the big powers, said the Secretary. "The Conference will be free to determine its own organization and procedures." Though the Conference would make only recommendations, "the members of the Council are committed, in drafting the final texts of the treaties, to consider the recommendations of the Conference and not to reject any of them arbitrarily."

In conclusion, the Secretary expressed a fundamental principle of the United States' peacemaking efforts. "We do not believe," he said, "in a peace based on a desire for vengeance. We believe in justice, charity, and mercy. If we act with charity and mercy, those we fear as enemies may become our friends."

IX.   The Five Draft Treaties

» «

THERE WAS A BASIC pattern in the drafts of the treaties which the Council had prepared for Italy, Rumania, Bulgaria, Hungary, and Finland and would offer to the 21-nation Paris Conference for its recommendations. Each of these treaties contained provisions on which the Council had reached agreement and, in the case of those issues on which the Council had not been able to reach a decision, alternative proposals. The members of the Council were committed to support, at the Conference, those provisions on which they had agreed.

Among the major provisions in each of the five draft treaties were clauses relating to territorial adjustments, protection of human rights, prevention of the rebirth of Fascist-type organizations, apprehension of war criminals and traitors, limitation of armed forces and armaments, prevention of German and Japanese rearmament, withdrawal of Allied forces of occupation, reparation, restitution, and compensation.

The problem of the administration and protection of the Free Territory of Trieste was dealt with in the Italian treaty. Points of view of various Council members on the question of the Danube were noted in the treaties with Rumania, Bulgaria, and Hungary.

A. Territorial Changes Affecting Italy

The treaty with Italy provided that—although the four powers had not come to an agreement on the exact frontier between Italy and Yugoslavia, nor on the exact frontier between Italy and the Free Territory of Trieste—Trieste and approximately 300 square miles of territory surrounding the important Adriatic port would be taken away from Italy. This area, the Free Territory of Trieste, would be placed under the international control of the Security Council of the United Nations.

Of the rest of Venezia Giulia—three quarters of the population of which was Yugoslav and one fourth Italian—about 3,000 square miles, or 85 percent, would be ceded to Yugoslavia, and some 500 square miles, or 15 percent, would remain Italian. Yugoslavia would get the predominantly Slavic hinterland and the coastal area including Pola, Rovigno, and Parenzo where the population was mixed. Yugoslavia

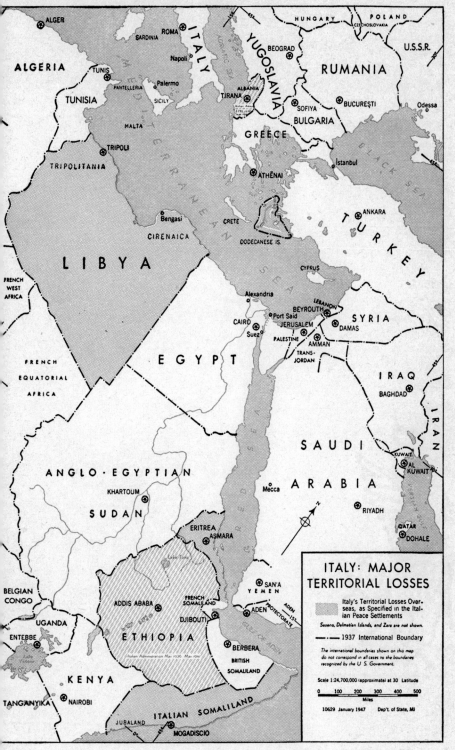

ITALY: MAJOR
TERRITORIAL LOSSES

Italy's Territorial Losses Overseas, as Specified in the Italian Peace Settlements

Sasseno, Dalmatian Islands, and Zara are not shown.

————— 1937 International Boundary

The international boundaries shown on this map
do not correspond in all cases to the boundaries
recognized by the U. S. Government.

Scale 1:24,700,000 (approximate) at 30° Latitude

0   100   200   300   400   500
Miles

10629 January 1947   Dep't of State, MI

734813°—47   (Face p. 30)

also would gain Isola Lunga and minor islands nearby and Zara and the Dalmatian Islands.

Italy would renounce in favor of Albania all claims to the island of Saseno, located at the mouth of the Albanian Bay of Vlonë.

The Dodecanese Islands would go to Greece.

The area adjacent to Bardonnèche, on the French-Italian border, would go to France. Tenda-Briga, on the same border, also would go to France. However, it was stipulated that industries and consumers on the Italian side of the border would have the right to buy from France, at reasonable rates, electric power produced in Tenda-Briga, which contained important hydro-electric developments.

The North African colony of Libya (Cyrenaica and Tripolitania) and the East African colonies of Eritrea and Italian Somaliland would come under a trusteeship decided upon by the Council within one year or, failing that, a trusteeship decided upon by the General Assembly of the United Nations.

B. Territorial Changes Affecting Rumania, Hungary, Finland, and Bulgaria

The treaty with Rumania fixed its frontiers in accordance with: (1) the Soviet-Rumanian Agreement of June 1940, which had been concluded before Rumania entered the war and which confirmed the Soviet Union's claim to Bessarabia and Northern Bucovina, and (2) the Bulgarian-Rumanian Agreement of August 1940, transferring the Southern Dobruja to Bulgaria.

The treaty with Hungary provided that this nation would return to Rumania the rich area of northern Transylvania, which is populated by 3,000,000 persons, most of whom are Rumanians. This area had been given to Hungary by Hitler during the war. Hungary also would lose to Czechoslovakia the Bratislava Bridgehead.

The treaty with Finland confirmed the Finnish-Soviet Armistices of 1940 and 1944 in respect of the cession to the Soviet Union of (1) the region of Petsamo, which stretches inland for approximately 140 miles and includes the warm-water Barents Sea port of Petsamo, an important harbor for trade with Atlantic Ocean countries; (2) another area of similar size midway on the border between the Arctic and the Baltic Seas; and (3) the province of Karelia, on the Gulf of Finland. In addition the Soviet Union would receive a fifty-year lease for the "use and administration of territory and waters for the establishment of a Soviet naval base in the area of Porkkala-Udd", which is in the Baltic and controls the approaches to the Gulf of Finland and Leningrad. (However, the Soviet Union would relinquish its lease on Hangö.)

The treaty with Bulgaria listed no losses in the territories of that nation and the acquisition of Southern Dobruja, from Rumania. But, it was stated, "this text should be considered as tentative in respect of the Greek-Bulgarian frontier," pending presentation of their points of view by Bulgaria and Greece to the Paris Conference or to the Council of Foreign Ministers.

C. Civil and Political Rights, Apprehension of War Criminals and Traitors, Limitation of Armed Forces and Armaments, Prevention of German and Japanese Rearmament, and Withdrawal of Forces of Occupation

Each of these five draft treaties contained:

(1) A "human rights" clause, which had its origin in an agreement at the Moscow Conference of Foreign Ministers in 1943, that such a clause, based upon the declarations of the Atlantic Charter, should be included in the treaty for Italy (b–2). In each treaty the wording of the clause, modeled upon the provisions of the Charter of the United Nations, was identical, except for the name of the nation concerned.

". . . shall take all measures necessary to secure to all persons under (its) . . . jurisdiction, without distinction as to race, sex, language or religion, the enjoyment of human rights and of the fundamental freedoms, including freedom of expression, of press and publication, of religious worship, of political opinion and of public meeting."

(2) A pledge that, in accord with the armistice agreements, none of these defeated countries would permit the resurgence within their territories of Fascist or other type organizations—whether political, military, or para-military—which proposed to deprive the people of their democratic rights.

(3) A pledge that the defeated nation would "take the necessary steps" to arrest and deliver to the Allies war criminals and citizens of the Allied and associated nations who had been traitors during the war.

(4) A pledge that none of the defeated countries would "possess, construct or experiment with" self-propelled or guided missiles. The extremely limited and specified armed forces permitted to each of the five countries "shall be designed to meet only tasks of internal character, local defence" of frontiers, and anti-aircraft defense. None of the nations might have bombing planes or planes adaptable to modern bombing.

(5) A pledge that each of these five defeated nations would cooperate with the Allied powers toward insuring that Germany and Japan would be unable to take steps outside German and Japanese territories toward rearmament.

(6) A statement that "All armed forces of the Allied and associated powers shall be withdrawn . . . as soon as possible and in any case not later than 90 days from the coming into force of the present treaty."

D. Reparation

Reparation would be in commodities, the Council decided.

Italy would pay to the Soviet Union reparation amounting to $100,000,000, according to the terms of the Council's agreement on this matter. Other claims for reparation from Italy, made by France, Yugoslavia, Greece, Albania, and Ethiopia, would be considered at the Paris Conference, "together with the means whereby and the extent to which they shall be met."

Bulgaria would pay reparation to Yugoslavia and Greece, for losses to them caused by "military operations and by the occupation by Bulgaria of the territory of those states." The amount and means of payment would be arranged after discussion with Yugoslavia and Greece.

Rumania would make reparation to the Soviet Union, to the amount of $300,000,000.

Hungary would make reparation in the amount of $200,000,000 to the Soviet Union, and $100,000,000 to Czechoslovakia and Yugoslavia. These three hundred million dollars' worth of commodities would be delivered by Hungary over a period of eight years, dating from January 20, 1945. (In regard to reparation from Hungary, the United States was not in complete accord with other members of the Council. It felt that the total was fixed too high, and reserved the right to reopen the question at the Paris Conference.)

Finland would pay reparation in the amount of $300,000,000 to the Soviet Union. This also would be payable over a period of eight years. (The United States did not participate in the Council's decisions on Finland, because it had not been at war with this nation.)

E. Restitution

In regard to restitution, the five draft treaties stated that there would be returned, in the shortest possible time and in good order, property removed by force or duress from United Nations' territories. Italy, Rumania, Bulgaria, Hungary, and Finland would:

(1) Bear the costs of such restitution.

(2) Provide, at their own expense, facilities for the search for and restitution of such property.

(3) Help to effect the return of such property held in other countries.

(4) Accept restitution claims up to six months after the treaties became effective.

The burden of identifying property and proving ownership rested on the claimants. The burden of proving that this property was not removed by force or duress rested on Italy, the three Balkan nations, and Finland.

F. Compensation

In all five treaty drafts lack of agreement was noted in relation to the amount of recompense for war damage, or property loss resulting from the war, to holdings of the United Nations or their nationals in the five countries. The United States, supported by the United Kingdom and France, proposed recompense, in the currency of the defeated nation, large enough "to enable the recipient to purchase similar property or to make good the loss or damage suffered." The Soviet Union took the position that since the countries which would receive reparation would be compensated only partially for their losses, compensation for war damage and loss to United Nations' property in the territory of the ex-enemy states also should be in part, to the extent of one third of the loss.

G. Administration and Protection of the Free Territory of Trieste

The Council also agreed that, in the treaty with Italy, it should be stated that the governor of the new Free Territory of Trieste would be appointed by the United Nations Security Council after consultations with both Yugoslavia and Italy. The government of the Free Territory would be democratic: all citizens would be permitted to vote; there would be freedom of religion, language, press, and schools; other fundamental human rights and freedoms also would be protected. But the Council could not agree on exactly how the integrity and independence of the Free Territory "shall be assured by the Security Council".

H. The Question of the Danube

In the treaties with the three Balkan nations, lack of agreement was noted in relation to a provision for freedom of navigation on the Danube, which President Truman had sought during the Potsdam Conference and which Secretary Byrnes also had sought to achieve at the various meetings of the Council.

The drafts of the treaties with Rumania, Bulgaria, and Hungary noted that the United States and the United Kingdom proposed: (1) free and open navigation on the Danube and tributaries, on terms of entire equality to the nationals, vessels of commerce, and goods of all states; and (2) in the establishment, administration, and operation of an international regime for the Danube River system, the three defeated countries should have voices equal to those of other member states.

These treaty drafts also noted the opinion of the Soviet Union, which held that the peace settlements with Rumania, Bulgaria, and Hungary could not solve the question of the Danube. Other Danubian states such as Czechoslovakia and Poland must participate. The Soviet Union proposed that there not be included in these three treaties any provision relating to the Danube.

I. The Attitude of the United States

In relation to the Council's progress in peacemaking, Secretary Byrnes made three points:

(1) "The drafts of treaties agreed upon," he said during his report on July 15 (a–7), "are not the best which human wit could devise. But they are the best which human wit could get the four principal Allies to agree upon. They represent as satisfactory an approach to the return of peace as we could hope for in this imperfect and war-weary world." He added in a statement which was broadcast on July 27 (a–8), "Unfortunately, in a world where national states jealously guard their sovereignty, there is no ideal peacemaking procedure."

(2) "Making the peace is a labor of compromise", the Secretary emphasized again in his statement of July 27. "The progress thus far is the product of compromise. There is no use to pretend that more compromises will not be necessary if we are to go the rest of the way. But the compromises we have reached and those I hope we will reach will be compromises intended to reconcile honest conflicts of opinion and not to secure selfish advantage for ourselves or others."

(3) A united America is necessary to peacemaking progress, the Secretary said on the afternoon of July 27 (a–8) as his plane prepared to take off from the Washington National Airport for Paris and the Conference. All Americans "are deeply conscious that if we as a nation are to exert our influence on the affairs of the world we must be united. The world cannot rely upon the cooperation of a divided America whose foreign policy is guided by temporary political expediency."

He commented on the difference between the post-war periods of World War I and World War II. "This time", Mr. Byrnes said, "there is no division between the Executive and the Congress as to the making of peace. This time there is no division between the great political parties as to the making of peace."

X. The Paris Conference, July 29–October 15, 1946

» «

A. Purpose and Participants

THE PARIS CONFERENCE to consider and make recommendations for the Council's draft treaties for Italy, the three Balkan nations, and Finland opened on Monday, July 29, 1946 in historic Luxembourg Palace in Paris.

As agreed by the Foreign Ministers of the Big Three during their meeting in Moscow in December 1945, the nations participating in the Paris Conference included the members of the Council of Foreign Ministers and all United Nations which actively had waged war with substantial force against the European members of the Axis. They numbered 21: the United States, United Kingdom, Soviet Union, France, China, Australia, Belgium, Byelorussian Soviet Socialist Republic, Brazil, Canada, Czechoslovakia, Ethiopia, Greece, India, the Netherlands, Norway, New Zealand, Poland, Ukrainian Soviet Socialist Republic, Union of South Africa, and Yugoslavia.

The United States Delegation included, again at Secretary Byrnes' request, Senators Connally and Vandenberg.

B. The Committees

The machinery of the Conference, which had been recommended by the Council during its recently concluded session and then confirmed by the Conference itself, included a General Commission, a Military Commission, a Legal and Drafting Commission, five political commissions, and two economic commissions. A two-thirds majority vote would be required for a commission's recommendation, but the minority also would have the right to express its views.

The General Commission, which never met, the Military Commission, and the Legal and Drafting Commission were composed of representatives of the 21 nations participating in the Conference.

The five political commissions were composed of representatives of the nations that were actively at war with the enemy country concerned. (There was one exception—France—which was admitted to all the committees but could vote only on the Italian treaty.)

The political commission for the Italian treaty had 20 members: the United States, the United Kingdom, Soviet Union, France, China,

Australia, Belgium, Byelorussian Soviet Socialist Republic, Brazil, Canada, Czechoslovakia, Ethiopia, Greece, India, the Netherlands, New Zealand, Poland, Ukrainian Soviet Socialist Republic, Union of South Africa, and Yugoslavia.

The political commission for the Rumanian treaty had 11 members: the United States, United Kingdom, Soviet Union, Australia, Byelorussian Soviet Socialist Republic, Ukrainian Soviet Socialist Republic, Czechoslovakia, India, New Zealand, Canada, and the Union of South Africa.

The political commission for the Bulgarian treaty had 12 members: The United States, United Kingdom, Soviet Union, Byelorussian Soviet Socialist Republic, Ukrainian Soviet Socialist Republic, Australia, Czechoslovakia, Greece, India, New Zealand, Union of South Africa, and Yugoslavia.

The political commission for the Hungarian treaty had 12 members: the United States, United Kingdom, Soviet Union, Byelorussian Soviet Socialist Republic, Ukrainian Soviet Socialist Republic, Australia, Canada, Czechoslovakia, India, New Zealand, Union of South Africa, and Yugoslavia.

The political commission for the treaty with Finland had 10 members: the United Kingdom, Soviet Union, Byelorussian Soviet Socialist Republic, Ukrainian Soviet Socialist Republic, Australia, Canada, Czechoslovakia, India, New Zealand, and the Union of South Africa.

One economic commission would be devoted to aspects of the Italian treaty. Its members were those 20 nations which were members of the political commission for the Italian treaty. The other economic commission would concern itself with the treaties with the three Balkan countries and Finland. Its members numbered 14: the United States, United Kingdom, Soviet Union, France, Australia, Byelorussian Soviet Socialist Republic, Canada, Czechoslovakia, Greece, India, New Zealand, Ukrainian Soviet Socialist Republic, Union of South Africa, and Yugoslavia.

C. Procedural Problems

Almost immediately the smaller nations opposed the recommendation of the Council that a two-thirds majority was needed for the Conference to make recommendations on the five draft treaties. The United States made clear that it had not been a party to, and did not consider itself bound by, this Council decision. The United States declared that it too believed that the Conference should have the right to adopt its own rules of procedure.

On August 9, after more than a week of discussion in the rules commission and seven and one-half hours of debate in plenary session, the Conference adopted a motion of the United Kingdom: proposals on the peace treaties which received the votes of a simple majority of the members of the Conference also would be received by the Council as Conference recommendations.

Another procedural problem involved the possibility that the Conference might overlap the next meeting of the United Nations General Assembly, scheduled to meet in New York on September 23. By August 29 the Conference had only barely begun discussing the terms of the draft treaties.

On September 8 the Council (excepting the United States) and the Belgian Delegate to the Conference, who also was chairman of the General Assembly, requested the Secretary-General of the United Nations to ascertain the views of all other members of the United Nations in regard to a postponement of the General Assembly to October 23. Though the United States did not join in this request it indicated that if a majority of the United Nations was in favor of such a postponement it would not oppose the step.

Shortly thereafter it was agreed by a majority of the United Nations that the General Assembly meeting should be postponed as requested. In the view of these nations it would have been difficult, if not impossible, to hold at the same time two such important international meetings as the Conference, which was concerned with making the peace, and the General Assembly, which was concerned with keeping the peace. There was a shortage of trained personnel in the Foreign Offices of most of the nations which were participating in the Conference, all of which were members of the General Assembly.

In order to speed the work of the Conference in its final stages, the Council offered and the Conference unanimously accepted suggestions to limit discussion of the treaties in order to conclude its work by October 15. The accelerated working schedule proposed for the commissions was formally adopted by the Conference on October 6. It also was agreed that each of the 21 delegations should be limited to one 30-minute speech on each of the five treaties, plus two 30-minute translation periods. Three days would be allowed for consideration of the Italian treaty and one day each for consideration of the treaties with Rumania, Bulgaria, Hungary, and Finland.

D. Substantive Issues

Some major substantive issues of the treaties considered by the Conference concerned: (1) the boundary of Trieste and between Italy and Yugoslavia; (2) the government of Trieste; (3) territorial adjustments other than those relating to Trieste and the boundary between Italy and Yugoslavia; (4) reparation; (5) compensation; (6) resti-

TRIESTE

BOUNDARIES

—·—·— 1937 International
••••••• Morgan Line
———— Post World War II

Scale 1 · 900,000

0   5   15   20
MILES

0   5   15   20
KILOMETERS

10631 January 1947, Dept. of State, MI

734813°—47   (Face p. 38)

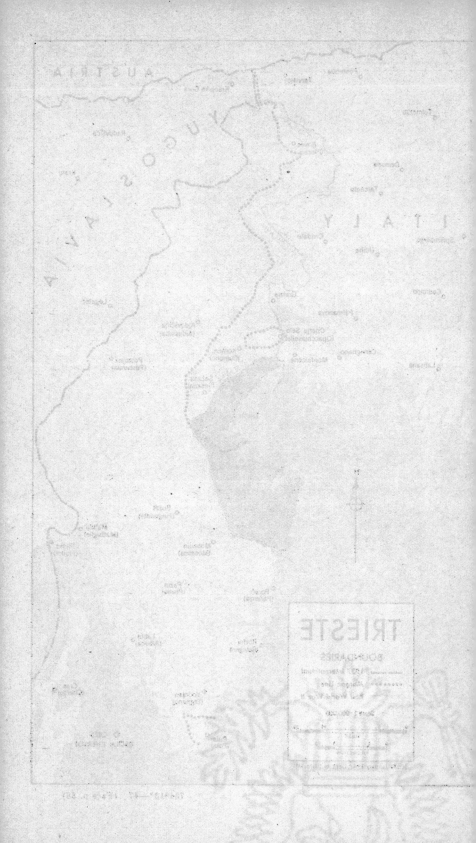

tution; (7) settlement of disputes arising from carrying out the provisions of the draft treaties; and (8) principles of foreign trade and navigation on the Danube.

1. The Boundary of Trieste and Between Italy and Yugoslavia

Difficult enough of solution, the complicated problems of Trieste and the Italo-Yugoslav boundary were further exacerbated by the Yugoslav Government's uncooperative attitude toward the Allied occupation forces in the western half of Venezia Giulia. Also, Yugoslavia declared during debate in the Italian Political Commission that it would not sign the Italian treaty if this treaty included the Council of Foreign Ministers' boundary agreements for Trieste and between Italy and Yugoslavia. Yugoslavia felt that it was entitled to all of Venezia Giulia.

However, on September 20 the delegates on the Italian Political Commission voted by a greater than two-thirds majority that the boundaries for Trieste and between Italy and Yugoslavia should be those upon which the Council of Foreign Ministers had agreed. In this and in all other Conference voting the members of the Council of Foreign Ministers stood by the decisions they had reached and included in the draft treaties.

A week later, on September 28, the full Conference upheld the Italian Political Commission's boundary decision by an equally large majority. Yugoslavia then announced that not only would it not sign the treaty with Italy but that it would never withdraw its troops from that part of northwest Istria which the Conference (and the Council) had decided should become part of the Free Territory of Trieste. The reaction of the Conference was to pass, by a narrow majority, a proposal offered by Senator Connally. According to this amendment, if Yugoslavia did not sign the Italian treaty, it would not receive from Italy reparation, territory, or other benefits to which it was entitled. Furthermore, on October 10 the Conference voted by a greater than two-thirds majority in favor of another United States proposal, namely that certain fundamental liberties be guaranteed to the inhabitants of territories ceded by Italy to Yugoslavia and other countries.

2. The Government of Trieste

The Council's draft treaty for Italy did not include an agreement on the precise form of the internationalized government to be established in the Free Territory of Trieste.

During Conference discussions on this question, the Soviet Union and Yugoslavia urged that: (1) in the Free Territory there should be an all-powerful popularly elected legislative assembly; and (2) the governor appointed by the Security Council of the United Nations should be restricted to a limited supervision. Yugoslavia also argued that Trieste should be placed within a Yugoslav customs, railway, monetary, and diplomatic union. The United States, the United Kingdom, and France thought that Trieste should be fully independent of its neighbors. Senator Connally, speaking on behalf of the United States (a–9), also felt that, while Trieste's popularly elected assembly should have a voice in governing the Free Territory, the final authority on all major decisions should rest with the governor appointed by the Security Council of the United Nations.

For three weeks a subcommittee composed of representatives of Australia, the United Kingdom, the United States, France, the Soviet Union, the Netherlands, Poland, and Yugoslavia attempted, unsuccessfully, to prepare an agreed statute for the administration of the Free Territory. Then, as a compromise, France submitted a proposal setting forth the minimum principles to be incorporated in the charter for the Free Territory. Although these principles did not go as far as the United States and the United Kingdom would have preferred with respect to the authority of the governor of Trieste and the authority of the United Nations, these principles were accepted by the United States and the United Kingdom as representing the maximum agreement possible. The Soviet Union and Yugoslavia, however, did not agree to the French compromise.

It was not until October 3 that the Italian Political Commission reached the point of voting on the principles of the charter for the administration of the Free Territory. During an all-night session, the Commission by more than a two-thirds majority adopted the principles of the French compromise proposal. However, within the framework of these principles, many of the details were left to be worked out by the Council of Foreign Ministers.

Both Yugoslavia (on October 8) and the Soviet Union (on October 9) criticized these decisions of the Italian Political Commission, and the Soviet Union urged once again that there be included in the Italian treaty a specific date by which all forces of occupation would be withdrawn from Trieste.

Yugoslavia said, in reference to the principles agreed upon by the Commission for administration of the Free Territory: "a new colony is being born in the heart of Europe". In reply the United Kingdom warned Yugoslavia not to "make the same mistake over Trieste" that Italy, following World War I, had made in seizing Fiume. France appealed to Yugoslavia to consider the advantages of what had been achieved at the Conference and to reconsider its decision not to sign the Italian treaty.

On October 10, after two sessions—the latter of which concluded at 3:30 a.m.—the Conference, again by a greater than two-thirds majority, upheld the Italian Political Commission's voting on the principles for the administration of the Free Territory. Also, during these sessions two proposals of the Soviet Union were approved by wide Conference majorities. The first proposal made the governor of Trieste responsible for the application of the Territory's statutes. The second provided that Trieste's legislative assembly be elected by proportional representation, in universal and secret suffrage.

3. Other Territorial Adjustments

Except for the boundaries of Trieste and between Italy and Yugoslavia, the 21-nation Conference had little difficulty in deciding that the five draft treaties should include the Council's agreements on territorial adjustments, many of which first were put on record in such documents as the armistices with Rumania and Finland. There was Conference discord, however, in relation to territorial questions involving Albania, Bulgaria, and Greece. Upon these problems the Council had reached no agreement in the draft treaties.

Greece proposed that the Conference should recommend to the Council that it give consideration to Greek claims to northern Epirus, a region within the present boundaries of Albania. Greece withdrew this proposal after discussion indicated that the Soviet Union and other states were opposed.

No conclusion was reached by the Conference in respect to Bulgarian claims in western Thrace, within Greece, or to Greek claims to a strip of Bulgarian territory along the present Greco-Bulgarian frontier, which was claimed for strategic reasons. The Conference recommended only—as in the case of the Franco-Italian and Italian-Yugoslav frontiers—that permanent fortifications and military installations along the border should be prohibited to the former enemy nation. The issue of territorial adjustments along the Greco-Bulgarian border was returned for final settlement to the Council, members of which were divided on this question. The Soviet Union, United States, and France believed that this border should remain unchanged. The United Kingdom was prepared to support the Greek claim on Bulgaria.

4. Reparation

The position of the United States on reparation was stated on August 3 by Assistant Secretary (later Under Secretary of State for Economic Affairs) William L. Clayton, a member of the United States Delegation to the Conference (a–10).

In a radio speech from Paris on the economic aspects of the five draft treaties he said that it was only natural "that the countries which suffered from aggression should demand reparations from the aggressor, but," he cautioned, "we must take into account the aggressor's ability to pay. It would do much more harm than good to exact so much of the former enemy that his economic and social structure would be so seriously weakened, as to endanger not only his own stability but that of his neighbors as well."

On September 11 Mr. Willard L. Thorp, a member of the United States Delegation to the Conference, who later was appointed Assistant Secretary of State, advised the other members of the Economic Commission for Italy that the United States, which had not been devastated in the war, was not interested in securing reparation for itself. Its interest in the question of Italian reparation lay in the accomplishment of "the difficult task of finding a fair and equitable balance between tremendous claims on the one hand and exceedingly limited resources on the other." He pointed out that "The imposition upon Italy of a crushing reparation burden would militate against the restoration of international economic stability, which is an essential basis for the maintenance of peace."

In subsequent deliberations on reparation by the economic commissions, the United States had occasion to reiterate these principles. On October 3 during a meeting of the Balkan Economic Commission, the United States in accord with its previous reservation proposed, unsuccessfully, that Hungarian reparation be reduced from $300,000,-000 to $200,000,000 worth of commodities.

By October 5 two economic commissions had voted on the distribution of reparation. According to the decision of the Italian Economic Commission, Italy would be obliged to pay reparation in the amount of $325,000,000 on the basis of current values to the Soviet Union, Yugoslavia, Greece, and Ethiopia. Claims of other states against Italy were to be met from Italian assets within their jurisdictions. The Balkan and Finnish Economic Commission recommended that Rumania pay $300,000,000 to the Soviet Union, Bulgaria pay $125,000,000 to Yugoslavia and Greece, Hungary pay $300,000,000, two thirds to the Soviet Union and one third to Yugoslavia and Czechoslovakia, and Finland pay $300,000,000 to the Soviet Union; these deliveries were to be valued, as provided in the armistice agreements, on the basis of 1938 prices.

The decisions of the economic commissions on reparation were upheld by the full Conference, which also approved an Australian proposal for a Reparation Commission to coordinate and supervise the treaty provisions for reparation to countries other than the Soviet Union. Despite a statement that statistical evidence pointed to an almost complete collapse of Hungarian industry, the United States again was unsuccessful in its attempt to get the Conference to reduce Hungarian reparation by one third. Nor did the Conference act on a United States request that Finland's reparation be reduced to $200,-000,000. Similarly, the Soviet Union did not achieve a Conference recommendation for Italian reparation to Albania.

5. Compensation

In his speech of August 3 (a–10), Mr. Clayton had discussed "claims arising out of the war." The five treaties under discussion, he said, should provide for just and prompt settlements, "so that the former enemy states may promptly resume normal economic relations with the United Nations."

During a meeting of the Italian Economic Commission on September 19, Mr. Thorp informed the Commission that the United States had reconsidered its position on compensation, in view of the burdens to be imposed on Italy by the treaty and the necessity to consider the effect of these burdens on the Italian economy. In view of the fact that many countries had a direct interest in the amount of compensation to be paid, the Commission should determine the amount but the United States would support a figure substantially below 100 percent. Later the United States specifically proposed that compensation should be fixed at 25 percent and was supported in this proposal by the Soviet Union. The French also supported a reduction from 100 percent and proposed 75 percent as a compromise. The Conference approved the French proposal, the United Kingdom voting with the majority, the Soviet Union voting against, and the United States abstaining.

6. Restitution

In regard to restitution, on which the Council of Foreign Ministers was in agreement, the Conference approved the draft treaty suggestions and added one of its own with which the Four Powers also were in agreement. This had to do with the restitution of objects of artistic, historical, or archeological value belonging to the cultural heritage of a member of the United Nations from whose territory such objects were removed, by force or duress, by representatives of these five defeated nations. It was recommended that, if any of these defeated nations could not make restitution of such objects, it would transfer to the injured nation concerned objects of the same kind as, and of substantially equivalent value to, the objects removed, so far as such objects were obtainable within their territories.

The Conference also recommended that the Rumanian and Hungarian treaties should contain special provisions for the restitution of their property—or for compensation when restitution was impossible—to the people of the Jewish faith or ancestry who had been subjected to racial or religious persecution in Rumania and Hungary.

7. Interpretation of the Treaties and Settlement of Disputes

The Council had agreed and the Conference recommended that the ambassadors or ministers of the Council powers (as specified in each treaty) for a period of 18 months should represent the Allies in dealing with the five former enemy countries in all matters concerning the execution and interpretation of the treaties.

In connection with the problem of settling disputes arising from carrying out provisions of the five treaties upon which the Council had not reached agreement the Conference recommended that:

(*a*) Disputes arising from carrying out the economic provisions of the Italian treaty should be settled according to an arbitration procedure proposed by the United States. This proposal was based upon a suggestion of the Italian Government.

(*b*) Disputes arising from carrying out other provisions of the Italian treaty which could not be settled by the ambassadors of the Council powers should be referred to the International Court of Justice. This was proposed by the United States, the United Kingdom, and France.

(*c*) Disputes arising from carrying out the economic provisions of the treaties with the three Balkan nations and Finland should be settled—as the United Kingdom had proposed—by a conciliation commission composed of representatives chosen by the parties to the dispute, with a third member to be chosen, if necessary, by the President of the International Court of Justice.

(*d*) Disputes arising from carrying out other provisions of the treaties with the three Balkan nations and Finland should be settled—according to the proposal of the United States and the United Kingdom—by the ambassadors or ministers of the Council powers as specified in the individual treaties or, if they failed to agree, by the International Court of Justice.

8. Principles of General Commercial Relations and Navigation on the Danube

In another part of his speech on August 3 (a–10), Mr. Clayton discussed the draft treaty "provisions of a temporary character governing trade and other economic relations between the former enemies and the United Nations" on which the Council had reached substantial agreement. Mr. Clayton said that these provisions, to be in force for a period of 18 months after the treaties became effective, would assure nondiscriminatory treatment: "the Allies will be entitled under these proposals to fair treatment of their trade and business enterprises only if they in turn grant similar treatment to the enemy states." He emphasized that "Agreement on any other basis could not long endure."

In regard to two major provisions relating to general commercial relations of Italy, the three Balkan nations, and Finland, on which the Council had not been able to reach a decision, the Conference recommended:

(*a*) The principle of most-favored-nation treatment should be applicable in branches of economic activity in which there were state monopolies. This was proposed by the United States, the United Kingdom, and France.

(*b*) Countries bordering on the three Balkan nations should not be exempted from the commercial relations provisions of the treaties with Rumania, Bulgaria, and Hungary. A proposal for such exemption had been made by the Soviet Union.

With regard to international commercial aviation rights in these five defeated countries, the Conference approved (i) a proposal of the United States for equality of opportunity and nondiscriminatory treatment and (ii) a proposal of the Netherlands that these five defeated countries should grant, on a reciprocal basis, the first two "freedoms of the air."

Whether there should be a provision in the treaties with Rumania, Bulgaria, and Hungary for freedom of navigation on the Danube was another question on which the Council, prior to the Paris Conference, had not been able to reach agreement. During a meeting of the Economic Commission for the Balkan nations and for Finland, the Soviet Union and the United States once again stated their positions.

The Soviet Union felt that the principle of international control of the Danube should not be established in these peace treaties. Senator Vandenberg, a member of this Economic Commission, contended that Danubian commerce could not prosper if it was "at the mercy of various uncoordinated, restrictive, and discriminatory administrations which respond to the local judgments of the eight national jurisdictions through which the Danube flows" (a–11). Furthermore, he pointed out that the Danube was a major factor in present and future German and Austrian economy, which was of interest to the United States as long as American occupation forces were maintained in Germany and Austria.

Following this exchange of views, a two-thirds majority of the Economic Commission voted on September 30 that there should be included in the treaties with the three Balkan nations a provision for the re-establishment of free navigation on the Danube. A two-thirds majority of the Commission voted also that a new international organization should be formed and given the responsibility of safeguarding this freedom of navigation.

These Commission recommendations were upheld by the Conference. On October 11, 15 out of the 21 nations of the Conference voted in favor of a clause in the three Balkan treaties for free navigation on the Danube. Fourteen out of the twenty-one nations voted that, six months after the three Balkan treaties became effective, there should be held, for the purpose of establishing the Danube's "new permanent international regime", an international conference, members of which would be Rumania, Bulgaria, Hungary, all other Danubian states, and the four nations of the Council of Foreign Ministers.

E. Germany: Core of the Peacemaking Problem

Germany, the major problem of peacemaking in Europe, was not on the agenda of and therefore could not be discussed at the Paris Conference. But on many occasions the question of Germany raised itself in the minds of the delegates of the 21 nations at the Conference.

Immediately preceding and during the period of the Conference spokesmen of the Great Powers made speeches and statements which drew Germany directly into the peacemaking picture. One of these speeches was made by Foreign Minister Molotov on July 10. Two others later were made by Secretary Byrnes on September 6 at Stuttgart in the American zone in Germany and on October 3 in Paris (b–21 and b–22).

1. Disarmament, Demilitarization, and Occupation

At Stuttgart before an audience including the Ministers President of the Länderrat (Council of German States) in the American zone, Secretary Byrnes made an important pronouncement in regard to Germany (b–21). Elaborating on remarks he had made in his report following the session of the Council in Paris, prior to the Conference, the Secretary declared:

"It is not in the interest of the German people or in the interest of world peace that Germany should become a pawn or a partner in a military struggle for power between the East and the West."

The four powers of the Council should sign a treaty to insure the disarmament and demilitarization of Germany for at least a generation. This goal, he said, was a "responsibility" accepted by the powers at Potsdam.

There would be no early withdrawal from Germany of American security forces. Nor would the United States withdraw before any other power or powers. "As long as there is an occupation army in Germany," Mr. Byrnes said, "the American armed forces will be a part of that occupation army."

2. Decentralization of Government

Stating that the Allies did not want Germany to "live under a dictatorship," Mr. Byrnes endorsed the principle of a decentralized, federal form of government for Germany. This would give partial autonomy to the German states.

The Secretary proposed that, first, a temporary provisional government of all Germany should be established, mainly through the efforts of the German people themselves. It "should not be hand-picked by other governments." This provisional government should draft "a federal constitution for Germany which, among other things, should insure the democratic . . . freedoms of all its inhabitants."

3. Economic Unification and Exports

With regard to economic policy, Mr. Byrnes declared: "if Germany is not to be administered as an economic unit as the Potsdam Agreement contemplates and requires", the level of industry should be raised. "Reparations from current production would be wholly incompatible with the levels of industry now established under the Potsdam Agreement." The United States "will not agree to the taking from Germany of greater reparations than was provided by the Potsdam Agreement."

The Secretary reiterated the United States' belief in the immediate need for the economic unification of Germany. He repeated, too, that "If complete unification cannot be secured, we shall do everything in our power to secure the maximum possible unification."

In supporting the case for German exports large enough to make her economy self-sustaining, the Secretary pointed out: "Germany is a part of Europe, and recovery in Europe, and particularly in the states adjoining Germany, will be slow indeed if Germany with her great resources of iron and coal is turned into a poorhouse."

4. Territorial Adjustments

In addition Mr. Byrnes spoke of Germany's boundaries.

At Yalta it had been agreed that the Soviet Union would extend its frontiers westward in Poland to the Curzon line. Poland would be compensated by Germany for this lost territory.

At Potsdam it was agreed that Germany should cede to the Soviet Union part of East Prussia. Poland was authorized to administer German territories eastward to the line of the Oder-Neisse rivers, pending a final decision on the degree of its territorial compensation at the conference which would negotiate peace with Germany.

The Secretary said, of Silesia and other eastern German areas under Polish administration, that the record of Potsdam clearly stated that "the heads of government did not agree to support at the peace settlement the cession of this particular area."

In connection with Germany's western boundaries, Mr. Byrnes indicated that the United States favored France's claim to the Saar, an important industrial area. But, he said, as far as the United States is aware, the Ruhr (an even more important industrial area) was German and should remain part of Germany. However, he added, the United States favored such control over all Germany, including the Ruhr, as might be necessary for international security.

Approximately two weeks later, on September 16, Foreign Minister Molotov said that territory east of the Oder-Neisse line, then under Polish administration, should be considered as permanently ceded to Poland by Germany. The United States, the United Kingdom, and the Soviet Union had committed themselves to this, said Mr. Molotov, through acceptance of evacuation of Germans from these territories.

France was particularly concerned with that part of Secretary Byrnes' Stuttgart speech which dealt with the Ruhr. France felt that a Germany which retained the Ruhr would mean a Germany able to rebuild for war.

On October 3 in a speech before the American Club in Paris, Secretary Byrnes reassured France (b–22). He pointed out that if the four powers signed the treaty proposed by the United States for the demilitarization and disarmament of Germany, then "the Ruhr could never become the arsenal of Germany or the arsenal of Europe." Mr. Byrnes also declared that the "peaceful, democratic, and disarmed Germany" which the United States was trying to help create is necessary "to the peace and security of France, our oldest ally, and is necessary to the peace and security of a free and prosperous Europe."

F. End of the Conference: Decisions of the Council for its Session in New York

Two and one-half months after the Conference opened, at the end of eight days of virtually round-the-clock discussion and voting, the delegates of the 21 nations, on October 14 as scheduled, ended their task of considering and making recommendations to the five draft treaties. But delegates of only 20 nations attended the last session on October 15 at which final approval was given to the Conference's official record.

Yugoslavia, which refused to participate in this last meeting, declared in a letter to the Conference: (1) it could not sign the Italian treaty unless changes were made in the main provisions affecting Yugoslavia but (2) it would continue to cooperate with its allies, "in order to find a solution reached by mutual consent . . ."

The meeting on October 15 brought to a close group participation by the smaller nations in the making of the peace treaties with Italy, Rumania, Bulgaria, Hungary, and Finland—for which purpose the Paris Conference had been called by the Council of Foreign Ministers. The smaller nations which had participated in the Conference not only had presented their views but also had offered a large number of treaty amendments, many of which were adopted or were taken as the basis of Conference recommendations to the Council.

Completion of its tasks by the Conference enabled the Council to decide on October 14—in accord with an agreement of the Foreign Ministers of the United States, the United Kingdom, and the Soviet Union, at Moscow in 1945—that it would begin meeting in New York City on November 4, 1946 to reconsider unresolved issues of the five draft treaties in the light of Conference recommendations. In this connection Secretary Byrnes said that he would do all he could to include in the five draft treaties every recommendation which had been approved by two thirds of the delegates at the Conference, "regardless of how the United States may have voted on that recommendation" at the Conference.

The Council also decided on October 14 that during its session in New York it would begin discussing a peace treaty with Germany.

G. Evaluation of the Conference

During the last days of the Conference, and for some time thereafter, several men who represented various of the attending nations estimated the value of the work done by the Conference.

Secretary Byrnes, Senator Vandenberg, Senator Connally, Foreign Minister Bevin, France's President-Foreign Minister Bidault, and Prime Minister Smuts of South Africa felt that the Conference had accomplished well the tasks assigned to it. In the opinion of Foreign Minister Molotov the "balance sheet" of the Conference "cannot be considered satisfactory". All of these spokesmen joined in deploring lack of unity among the powers.

The United States, the United Kingdom, and France on the one hand and the Soviet Union on the other did not see eye-to-eye on specific points relating to the five draft treaties. They differed, also, regarding immediate problems in Germany and on the making of a prompt peace with Austria. In addition there was lack of agreement on several matters not directly involved in the making of the peace treaties but which, nonetheless, affected the general climate in which the Conference took place. These included differences over: (1) the economic situation in Hungary; (2) the political situation in Rumania, Bulgaria, and Poland; and (3) administration of the Dardanelles and Black Sea straits which, within Turkish boundaries, connected the Mediterranean and Black Seas.

1. Relations Between the United States and the Soviet Union

The condition of relations between the United States and the Soviet Union was discussed by Secretary Byrnes on October 18 (a–12) and by Senator Vandenberg on October 19 (a–13) during reports the two men made to the American people on the Paris Conference.

Admitting concern over the "continued if not increasing tension between us and the Soviet Union", the Secretary said that, between the two nations, there were "real and deep differences in interest, in ideas, in experience, and even in prejudices". These differences could not be reconciled "by any single act of faith". A real understanding would take a long time and require fairness and justice on both sides.

Declaring that the United States would continue to seek friendship with the Soviet Union "on the basis of justice and the rights of others, as well as ourselves, to opinions and ways of life which we do not and cannot share", the Secretary strongly urged the American people not to fall into the error of thinking that war was inevitable between the Soviet Union and the United States.

"It is that idea of the inevitability of conflict that is throttling the economic recovery of Europe", Mr. Byrnes said. "It is that idea that is causing artificial tensions between states and within states."

Developing this theme, Senator Vandenberg said: "Russia does not want war. America does not want war. We both are in the United Nations to prevent war."

Urging the American people to unite behind the bipartisan foreign policy of "friendly firmness" toward the Soviet Union, which Secretary Byrnes was carrying out, Senator Vandenberg stated that he had "no illusions about the perilous difficulties we confront. But I want to make equally plain that I am not surrendering to pessimism."

Similarly looking to the future without pessimism was Foreign Minister Molotov. On October 21 as he arrived in the United States to attend the meeting of the United Nations General Assembly and, later, the Council of Foreign Ministers, the Soviet Union's Foreign Minister declared:

"I am sure that important tasks now before the United Nations can be successfully solved and that any differences can be overcome given good will and the real desire to achieve mutual understanding." The

Soviet Union also would help to insure that the Council "is successful in accomplishing the interests of strengthening peace and the well-being of peoples, great and small."

2. International Relations in General

A broad appeal to the nations to settle their differences and to end the fears and rumors of another war was made by President Truman on October 23 (b–23), as he opened the meeting of the General Assembly in New York.

Stating that permanent peace could be built only upon the foundation of peace settlements which "rest upon the four essential freedoms" of the Atlantic Charter and the United Nations Charter, the President pointed out that "freedom from fear" meant, among other things, freedom from fear of war.

In connection with the five draft treaties—which had been considered by the Conference and which the Council of Foreign Ministers hoped to put into final form at their meeting beginning on November 4—Mr. Truman declared that agreements would not be lasting if they were reached "at the expense of the security, independence, or integrity of any nation." The United States, said the President, would continue to seek agreements that: (1) were "just to all states, large and small"; (2) "uphold the human rights and fundamental freedoms"; and (3) "do not contain the seeds of new conflicts".

During a luncheon that same day in honor of the delegates to the General Assembly, Secretary Byrnes commented to his colleagues in the work of peacemaking and peacekeeping:

"So long as we as individuals can work together and live together as friends there is no reason why the governments we represent cannot work together and live together as friends."

He offered a toast, which was received with wide enthusiasm:

"Not to any government, not to any nation . . . to peace and understanding and to the peoples of the world . . . our one world."

XI. Meeting of the Council of Foreign Ministers in New York, November 4–December 12, 1946

» «

A. Participants

A T 4 P. M. ON November 4, 1946 with Secretary Byrnes as chairman, the Council of Foreign Ministers began its session in New York— in a suite of offices which towered 37 floors above the heart of Manhattan Island. The participants were Secretary Byrnes, Foreign Minister Bevin, Foreign Minister Molotov, and France's Deputy Foreign Minister, Couve de Murville. President-Foreign Minister Bidault was unable to attend because of national elections which were held in France during the period of the Council session. Once again Senators Connally and Vandenberg had acceded to Mr. Byrnes' request that they advise him during a Council session.

B. Goal

The goal that the Council set for its session in New York was resolution of those issues of the five draft treaties on which the four powers had not yet reached agreement. In this connection, the United States had committed itself to support recommendations which had received the votes of two thirds of the delegates at the Paris Conference. The United Kingdom, France, and the Soviet Union had not committed themselves to such support.

C. Hope

The hope of the Council was that it would resolve those issues within three weeks. Then the Council would begin discussing a peace settlement with Germany, the crux of the problem of peace in Europe.

D. Problems and Points of View: Completion of the Final Treaties With Italy, Rumania, Bulgaria, Hungary, and Finland

With regard to the five draft treaties, the first decisions reached by the Council were procedural. (1) It would discuss questions on which agreement still was lacking as those questions came up within each individual treaty. (2) The treaties would be taken up in the "Potsdam" order—first Italy, then Rumania, Bulgaria, Hungary, and Finland. (3) If the Council should find itself approaching an impasse on any issue it should set that issue aside and come back to it only after it had reached as full agreement as possible on the other issues in the five draft treaties.

The major substantive issues of the five draft treaties which were to be resolved by the Council concerned:

1. The Government of the Free Territory of Trieste

It had been agreed that Trieste should be administered by a governor appointed by the Security Council of the United Nations, the five permanent members of which were the United States, the United Kingdom, the Soviet Union, France, and China.

The United States, United Kingdom, France, and a two-thirds majority of the Paris Conference believed that the governor of Trieste should have adequate powers and be subject to the Security Council rather than to a popularly elected legislative assembly by Trieste, a majority of the population of which was Yugoslav. The Soviet Union believed that the governor should be responsible to Trieste's assembly and that he should merely report to the Security Council.

Prior to reaching agreement on this complicated issue—which was the subject of drawn-out and arduous discussions held between November 4 and December 11—the Council listened to the views of Italy and Yugoslavia, the two nations primarily concerned with the problem of Trieste.

The spokesman for Italy, Signor Alberto Tarchiani, Ambassador to the United States, charged that the Italian draft treaty was not in keeping with the principles of the Atlantic Charter and that it practically ignored Italian co-belligerency during the war. He said that Italy could not voluntarily accept the settlement proposed for Trieste by the Council and the Paris Conference, "because of its human injustice, its fractional inefficiency, its denial of democratic principles and its failure to carry out the hopes held forth to all nations by the Atlantic Charter."

Though the spokesman for Yugoslavia, Foreign Minister Stanoje Simic, also criticized the proposed settlement for Trieste, his Government relaxed the adamant opposition it had maintained during the Paris Conference against the Italian treaty. Yugoslavia still argued that it should be given that part of Venezia Giulia, including the city of Gorizia, which the Council and a substantial majority of the Conference had agreed was Italian and should remain Italian. But Yugoslavia now agreed that the governor of Trieste should be appointed by the Security Council, no longer insisting that he should be a Yugoslav.

Nor did it continue to insist that it should be permitted to keep a garrison in Trieste, and it dropped its claim to the railroad junction city of Tarvisio.

After many hours of painstaking and often laborious discussion the Council had agreed by November 16:

(1) That the governor of Trieste should be the authority to declare when there was a state of emergency in the Free Territory; and

(2) How, in such a situation, the governor should intervene and take over control of Trieste's police force and executive powers.

On November 18, it decided that:

(3) The governor should have the determining voice in appointing or dismissing the police chief of Trieste;

(4) The governor might require Trieste's popularly elected council to suspend administrative measures which, in his view, conflicted with his responsibilities as defined in the statute being drawn for the government of Trieste;

(5) The governor could propose legislation to the local council in matters affecting his responsibilities as defined in the statute; and

(6) The governor's responsibilities should include insuring that public order and security are maintained by the government of Trieste in accordance with the statute, constitution, and laws of the Free Territory.

On November 25, it agreed that:

(7) The governor could order emergency measures in order to protect the human rights of the inhabitants of Trieste.

On November 26, it agreed that:

(8) Ninety days after the governor was appointed he would decide whether or not the forces of occupation could be withdrawn safely from the Free Territory. If he decided that conditions warranted a withdrawal, he would leave it up to the American, British, and Yugoslav commanders on the spot to determine the exact date and the physical details. If he decided that the troops could not be withdrawn safely he would report this decision to the United Nations Security Council.

(9) Upon ratification of the Italian peace treaty, the number of troops in Trieste would be reduced to 5,000 each for Yugoslavia, the United Kingdom, and the United States, each of which at the time of this agreement had approximately 15,000 men in the area.

(10) The governor would order elections in Trieste within four months of the ratification of the Italian treaty. In the interim period

THE DANUBE RIVER

— · — · — International Boundary—1937

Regensburg River Port

Scale 1 : 7,120,000

0   50   100   150
MILES

0   50   100   150
KILOMETERS

10630   January 1947, Dept. of State, MI

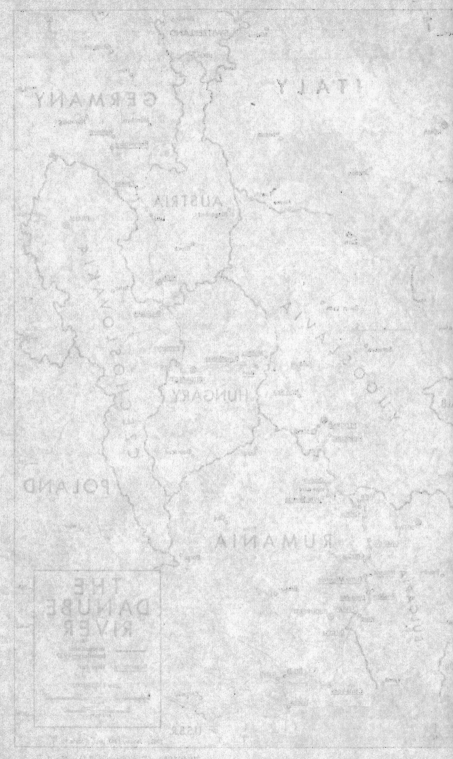

TALLINN

ESTONIA

SWEDEN

RIGA

LATVIA

LITHUANIA

Niemen

Kaliningrad   EAST   KAUNAS   Vil'nyus
                                          (Wilno)
Danzig   Braunsberg   PRUSSIA
POLISH   Goldap
         POLISH ADMINISTRATION
Stettin   Grodno
POLISH
UNDER

BERLIN   Poznań   Brest
ALLIED   Warta   WARSZAWA
                  Wisła
CUPATION   ADMINISTRATION   Bug
                  Odra

Elbe

PRAHA   Kraków   Rava - Russkaya
                           Wisła   L'vov
CZECHOSLOVAKIA   Przemyśl   (Lwow)
                           Solina
Danube   Dnostr

AUSTRIA   WIEN   Bratislava   Uzhgorod
                               (Užhorod)
          HUNGARY   RUMANIA

POLAND

▬▬·▬ 1937 International Boundary   ▬▬▬ Post World War II Boundary

Scale 1:6,810,000

0   100   200   300
              Miles

The northern part of East Prussia and Lithuania, Latvia and Estonia are administered by the U.S.S.R.; the Government of the United States
has not recognized the incorporation of Lithuania, Latvia and Estonia into the Soviet Union.

The international boundaries shown on this map do not correspond in all cases to the boundaries recognized by the U. S. Government.

526 January 1947   Department of State, MI

734813°—47   (Face p. 54)   No. 2

the governor, after consultations with Yugoslavia and Italy, would appoint a local council of government, which would administer the affairs of the Free Territory until the elected council could begin to function. Also, during the interim period, military rule would continue in Trieste, except in regard to those articles of the permanent statute which could be applied during this brief time.

On November 29, the Council further agreed that:

(11) Trieste citizenship should be refused to members of the former Italian fascist police who had not been exonerated by "competent authorities," including the Allied military authorities. The popularly elected assembly of Trieste should determine—for non-residents who might want to acquire citizenship in Trieste—the conditions of citizenship and include these conditions in the new Trieste constitution.

By December 6, the Council also had agreed that:

(12) Italy and Yugoslavia, as states primarily interested in Trieste, in agreement with the Free Territory might negotiate agreements providing for joint operation of the railways running in the direction of their own territories respectively;

(13) Freedom of transit should be assured to goods transported by railroad between the Free Territory and the states which it serves without discrimination or customs duties and charges;

(14) Yugoslavia and Italy should have free docking facilities in the area of the Free Territory;

(15) Trieste would be permitted to act as the maritime agency for merchant vessels of Austria, Czechoslovakia, Hungary and Switzerland, land-locked nations whose foreign trade would be dependent to an important extent upon the port of Trieste;

(16) Trieste would be permitted representation on international organizations such as the United Nations Economic and Social Council;

(17) During the provisional administration of Trieste and prior to the entry into force of the permanent statute for the government of Trieste, the governor would have the power not only to appoint but also to remove a member of the local council of government, if he felt it necessary;

(18) The United Nations should be asked to pay the salaries and expenses of the governor of Trieste and his staff; and

(19) The Security Council of the United Nations should be requested formally to accept the responsibility for naming the governor and, through him, for operating the government of Trieste.

The last remaining problems involved in the issue of Trieste were resolved during a meeting on December 11. The Council then decided that:

(20) A four-power commission should be sent to Trieste to make an on-the-spot investigation of (a) the financial requirements for operating the government of the Free Territory during the initial months of its existence and (b) problems in connection with the setting up of the Free Territory's currency and customs regime.

(21) The exact frontiers of Trieste should follow the line agreed on by the Council and approved by the Paris Conference.

(22) There should be a director over the international port of Trieste and an international port commission, members of which would include the United States, the United Kingdom, the Soviet Union, and France.

With these agreements the Council substantially resolved the issue of Trieste. Since September 1945, it had been the most vexing issue of the Italian treaty which, in turn, had presented the most difficult problems of the five draft treaties.

2. Settlement of Disputes Arising From Carrying out Provisions of the Treaties

The problem of how to settle disputes arising from carrying out provisions of the treaties with Italy, the three Balkan nations, and Finland was settled during the session in New York when the Council agreed that:

(a) Disputes arising under the economic clauses of these five treaties should be referred to a Conciliation Commission composed of representatives of the parties concerned, with provision for the appointment of a third member if necessary.

(b) First attempts to resolve disputes arising under other clauses of the five treaties should be made by representatives of the government of the United Nation concerned and the government of the former enemy nation concerned. Representatives of the two parties to the dispute would be equal in number and on an equal footing. If, within three months, they could not settle the dispute, either government would have the right to ask that a third party be involved. If agreement could not be reached on the choice of a third participant in the settling of the dispute, either government would have the privilege of asking the Secretary-General of the United Nations to appoint a third party. This three-party conciliation board would be the final authority for settling the dispute.

3. Freedom of Navigation on the Danube

As the problem of the Danube came up for discussion, it was the opinion of the United States, the United Kingdom, France, and a two-thirds majority of the Paris Conference that there should be included in the treaties with the three Balkan nations a provision for freedom of navigation on this important trade artery which stretches across Europe from Germany to the Black Sea. These three powers and the Paris Conference believed, also, that the Council, within six months of the time that the treaties with Rumania, Bulgaria, and Hungary became effective, should call an international conference which would set up an international authority to regulate Danubian traffic. Members of the international authority on Danubian traffic would include the members of the Council and the nations along whose borders or through which the Danube flowed.

The Soviet Union was not convinced that: (a) navigation on the Danube was a subject for inclusion in the treaties with the three Balkan nations and (b) questions involving this important trade artery were the concern of other than the eight Danubian nations, which were Germany, Austria, Czechoslovakia, Hungary, Yugoslavia, Rumania, Bulgaria, and the Soviet Union.

This question was resolved on December 4, when the Council agreed that the treaties with Rumania, Bulgaria, and Hungary should include a provision relative to free navigation on the Danube. It was decided also, though outside the framework of the three peace settlements, that, within six months after the treaties with these Balkan nations became effective, the Council would call an international conference to set up a Danube navigation authority.

4. Principles of General Commercial Relations

At New York the Council accepted the Conference recommendations with regard to the treaty provisions on general commercial relations, with the exception that all reference to state monopolies was deleted. Italy, the three Balkan nations, and Finland—during the first 18 months after the treaties became effective—were committed to extend, on a reciprocal basis, most-favored-nation treatment in their trade relations with United Nations. These five defeated nations also were committed to grant national and most-favored-nation treatment to United Nations nationals engaging in business activity within their jurisdictions.

5. Reparation

The Council's discussions in New York on reparation for the most part had to do with the Italian and Bulgarian treaties.

In regard to Italian reparation, the United States, the United Kingdom, France, and a majority of the Paris Conference believed that Italy should pay equal amounts to Greece and Yugoslavia. The Soviet Union contended that Italy should pay more reparation to Yugoslavia than to Greece. The Soviet Union thought also that Italy should pay reparation to Albania, on which question the three other powers of the Council and the Paris Conference had reached no positive conclusion.

In regard to Bulgarian reparation, the United States, the United Kingdom, France, and a majority of the Paris Conference had agreed that Bulgaria should pay a total reparation amounting to $125,000,000 to Greece and Yugoslavia. The United States, the United Kingdom, and France maintained that Greece and Yugoslavia should get equal amounts. The Soviet Union thought that: (a) there should be a reduction in the amount of reparation Bulgaria should pay and (b) Bulgaria should pay more to Yugoslavia than to Greece.

In regard to Hungarian reparation, the Soviet Union, the United Kingdom, France, and a majority of the Conference were in agreement. But the United States thought that Hungary should pay one third less than the amount agreed upon.

In regard to Rumanian reparation, the Council and the Paris Conference were in agreement.

In regard to Finnish reparation, the Soviet Union, the United Kingdom, France, and a majority of the Paris Conference were in agreement. The United States, which was not involved in Council decisions on this issue as it had not been at war with Finland, voiced the opinion that Finnish reparation should be reduced by one third, to bring it into just relation to reparation paid by wealthier, larger nations such as Rumania.

The issue of reparation was resolved by December 4, when the Council decided, upon the basis of a compromise proposal offered by France, that:

Italy would pay in commodities and over a period of seven years: $125,000,000 to Yugoslavia, $105,000,000 to Greece, $100,000,000 to the Soviet Union, $25,000,000 to Ethiopia, and $5,000,000 to Albania.

Rumania would pay in commodities and over a period of eight years $300,000,000 to the Soviet Union. In this connection agreement finally was reached on a question which long had been debated in the Conference and the Council, namely, whether special provisions should be included relating to the prices paid by the Rumanian Government for goods acquired from Allied nationals and delivered as reparation. Although the Council decided not to include in the Rumanian treaty a guaranty that fair prices would be paid for such goods, it did agree to establish procedures by which there could be equitably settled disputes over such prices.

Hungary would pay in commodities and over an eight-year period $200,000,000 to the Soviet Union, and $100,000,000 to Czechoslovakia and Yugoslavia. The two latter nations agreed later that, of this amount, Yugoslavia should get $70,000,000 and Czechoslovakia $30,000,000.

Bulgaria would pay in commodities and over an eight-year period $45,000,000 to Greece and $25,000,000 to Yugoslavia.

Finland would pay in commodities over an eight-year period $300,-000,000 to the Soviet Union.

6. Compensation to Nationals of the United Nations for Wartime Damage to or Destruction of Their Property in Italy, Rumania, Bulgaria, Hungary, and Finland

As discussion began on compensation, France and a majority of the Paris Conference thought that the five draft treaty nations should pay 75 percent of the amount it would take United Nations nationals to repair wartime damage to their property in Italy, Rumania, Bulgaria, Hungary, and Finland. The United States felt that the amount of such compensation should be fixed at 25 percent. The Soviet Union supported this figure. The United Kingdom maintained its position in favor of full compensation.

After a series of discussions which began during the first week of the New York session, the Council reached a decision on compensation on December 4 during the same meeting at which it resolved the problem of reparation. The Council agreed on a compromise solution offered by France that Italy, Rumania, Bulgaria, Hungary, and Finland should pay 66⅔ percent compensation.

7. The Boundary Between Greece and Bulgaria

In regard to the boundary between Greece and Bulgaria on which the Paris Conference had reached no decision, the United States, the Soviet Union, and France held that no changes should be made. The United Kingdom thought that Bulgaria should cede to Greece a small area in the vicinity of the Greek port of Salonika, which would make this Greek boundary more defensible.

This issue first came up before the Council on September 11 and was settled on December 3. It was agreed that: (*a*) no changes should be made in the boundary between Greece and Bulgaria and (*b*) Bulgaria could build no fortifications on its side of the Greek frontier.

8. The Italo-Austrian Agreement on the South Tyrol

At New York the Foreign Ministers discussed the recommendation of the Paris Conference that the Italian treaty should include an agreement independently reached by Italy and Austria on the South Tyrol, a region within Italy bordering on Austria, the population of which was largely of Austrian descent.

This agreement stemmed from a suggestion of the Council made prior to the Paris Conference that Italy and Austria should settle between them a number of minor economic problems connected with traffic across the Tyrolean border. The Italians and the Austrians, independently of the Conference, reached a wide-ranging agreement which: (*a*) guaranteed equal rights to the German-speaking population of the South Tyrol; (*b*) freed trade and travel from many irritating restrictions; and (*c*) in general, made this border unimportant as a source of international friction.

Hailing this agreement as one of the most constructive achievements of peacemaking since the end of World War II and expressing the hope that it would become a pattern for removing tensions in other disputed frontier areas of Europe, the United States, the United Kingdom and France (and the Paris Conference) urged that it be included in the Italian treaty. The Soviet Union, while it conceded that Italy and Austria had the right to make such an agreement, believed that there should be no reference to it in the treaty.

Agreement was reached on this question on December 3. The Council decided that signatories to the Italian treaty should take note that an Italo-Austrian agreement had been reached on the South Tyrol and that the provisions of this agreement should be set forth as an annex to the treaty with Italy. Although no expression of opinion in regard to the agreement would be contained in the treaty its inclusion as an annex at least implied approval.

E. Decisions Connected with Signing the Treaties, February 10, 1947

The peace settlements with Italy, the three Balkan nations, and Finland (b–24) virtually were completed by the Council on December 6. It would take at least a month more, the Foreign Ministers then agreed, to compile official English, Russian, and French texts. Therefore, they decided, these five treaties should be signed on February 10, 1947.

On that date, in Paris, representatives of the nations which had taken part in the Paris Conference and representatives of Italy, Rumania, Bulgaria, Hungary, and Finland would affix their signatures to the peace settlements which had been concluded by the Allies after more than a year's intensive discussion.

The treaties would come into force immediately upon ratification by the Allied states which had signed the respective armistices and—in the case of Italy—France.

F. *Germany and Austria*

On December 7, the fifth anniversary of the Japanese attack on Pearl Harbor, the Council began preliminary discussions on the basic question of peacemaking in Europe—a treaty with Germany.

1. Economic Unification of the American and British Zones in Germany

Meanwhile, on December 2 the United States and the United Kingdom had signed their bilateral agreement for the economic unification of their two zones of occupation in Germany (b–25) : thereby, the two Council powers considered that they could make this area self-sustaining within three years. As they signed this agreement, the United States and the United Kingdom again stressed that it was their hope that discussions would follow with the Soviet Union and France which would lead to economic unification of all Germany.

2. Decision for the Council Meeting in Moscow Beginning March 10, 1947

The first major decision reached by the Council in connection with the task of drawing up a peace settlement with Germany was the time and place of its next session. On December 9 Foreign Minister Molotov offered and the Council accepted an invitation to meet in Moscow. The Foreign Ministers were assured that, despite the difficult housing situation in the Soviet capital city, everything possible would be done to find room for visiting correspondents, and that these correspondents would be able to report the Council's activities in Moscow just as well as they had in Paris and in New York. The Council then agreed that the forthcoming session should begin on March 10, 1947.

3. Decision for the Appointment of Special Deputies for the German and Austrian Treaties

Other Council decisions reached on December 11 concerned what should be done in the interval between the New York session and the Moscow session to assist the Foreign Ministers in preparing peace settlements with Germany and Austria. It was agreed that:

(*a*) Special deputies should be appointed immediately to study the problems of a peace settlement with Germany. They would begin work in London on January 14, 1947. One of their first tasks would be to hear the views of Germany's smaller neighbors, Czechoslovakia, Poland, the Netherlands, Belgium, and Luxembourg, and possibly other countries, on what the German peace terms should include.

(*b*) Special deputies should be appointed immediately to start drafting a treaty with Austria. They also would meet in London in January 1947, and one of their first tasks would be to hear the views of Austria's neighbors on what should be included in an Austrian peace treaty.

4. The Agenda for the Council Session in Moscow

Finally, it was agreed on December 11 that the agenda for the Council session in Moscow should include:

(*a*) A series of reports from the Allied Control Authority in Germany. Within this series there would be a report by the Control Authority on its work in the fields of demilitarization, denazification, democratization, reparation, and relating to economic principles in the occupation zones. Another report would deal with the establishment of central administrative agencies and other problems concerned with the economic, financial, and political situation in Germany. Still another report would deal with the "liquidation of Prussia", the decentralization of what had been the most militaristic and powerful of the German states.

(*b*) The form and scope of the provisional government to be set up by the Allies in Germany.

(*c*) The preparation of the German peace treaty itself, including decisions on the frontiers and on the future status of the Ruhr and the Rhineland.

(*d*) The long-term disarmament and demilitarization of Germany— in accord with the treaty for such a purpose which the United States had offered the other powers during the Paris meetings of the Council of Foreign Ministers.

(*e*) The consideration of a report on the European coal situation. The lack of coal was the major reason for Europe's halting progress toward reconstruction and recovery, which in turn was causing much suffering and political instability throughout the whole continent.

In addition, the Council decided that although it would not place on the agenda the question of a reduction in the number of Allied occupation troops in Europe, that problem might be discussed if it were brought up. In this connection Secretary Byrnes had proposed that the forces of occupation in Germany, Poland, Austria, Hungary, and Rumania by April 1, 1947 should be reduced to 620,000 men, including 240,000 troops of the Soviet Union; that by April 1, 1948 there should be a further reduction of between 25 percent and 33⅓ percent, "subject to such earlier withdrawal from Austria, Hungary and Rumania as may be required by the Austrian treaty."

G. The Basic Continuity of the Foreign Policy of the United States

The Council's historic peacemaking session in New York City came to a close on December 12, 1946. Nearly 15 months to a day after the Council had sat down to its first meeting in London, the final settlements had been drafted for Italy, Rumania, Bulgaria, Hungary, and Finland.

In his report on the Council session in New York, the important part played by the smaller nations in the preparation of the peace settlements with Italy, the three Balkan nations, and Finland was noted by Charles E. Bohlen, Special Assistant to the Secretary of State, who had participated in many of the international peacemaking and peacekeeping conferences (a–14). Mr. Bohlen pointed out:

"In effect the final texts of these treaties reveal that on the majority of issues final agreement was based upon the recommendations returned to the Council of Foreign Ministers by the Paris Conference."

This report also singled out, as perhaps an equally important accomplishment of the session in New York, the preparatory work which had been done in connection with the task of drafting peace treaties with Germany and Austria.

It was the general opinion that, if there was a continuance of the spirit of cooperation and compromise which had characterized the New York session of the Council, the doubts and disorders which had alarmed the world since the end of World War II would be sensibly diminished.

Contributing not a little to these achievements in peacemaking and to favorable conditions for the future was a statement on the basic continuity of United States foreign policy, which had been made by Senator Vandenberg, a leader of the Republican Party and, as a result of the congressional elections on November 5, the incoming chairman of the Foreign Relations Committee of the Senate. In the speech which he delivered to the delegates of the nations of the General Assembly on November 8, Senator Vandenberg declared:

"Regardless of what political regime sits in Washington, you can count upon the whole-hearted cooperation of the government of the United States in striving, through the United Nations, for a system of mutual defense against aggression and for organized peace with justice in a better, safer world."

On January 11, 1947, a few days after President Truman reluctantly had accepted the resignation of Secretary Byrnes, whose health had been severely taxed by the labors of his office and long years of public service, Mr. Byrnes made his last major speech as Secretary of State.

Reviewing the accomplishments, objectives, and responsibilities of peacemaking and peacekeeping, Mr. Byrnes declared at the Twenty-first Annual Institute of the Cleveland Council on World Affairs (a–15):

". . . we would never have made the progress that we did during the last year if the American people had not been united on a foreign policy.

"For the past year our foreign policy has not been the policy of a political party; it has been the policy of the United States."

Drawing on his vast and hard-won experiences in the project of making the peace, Secretary Byrnes declared in conclusion:

"I admit that during the past year there were times when I was deeply discouraged. Our repeated efforts to achieve cooperation in a peaceful world seemed to be meeting only with constant rebuff. But we persisted in our efforts with patience and with firmness.

"Today I am happy to say that I am more confident than at any time since V–J Day that we can achieve a just peace by cooperative effort if we persist 'with firmness in the right as God gives us the power to see the right.' "

Appendixes

APPENDIX 1

Excerpts From Report of the President to the Nation on the Potsdam Conference, Delivered on August 9, 1945

. . . .

BEFORE WE MET at Berlin, the United States Government had sent to the Soviet and British Governments our ideas of what should be taken up at the Conference. At the first meeting our Delegation submitted these proposals for discussion. Subjects were added by the Soviet and British Governments, but in the main the Conference was occupied with the American proposals.

Our first non-military agreement in Berlin was the establishment of the Council of Foreign Ministers.

The Council is going to be the continuous meeting-ground of the five principal governments, on which to reach common understanding regarding the peace settlements. This does not mean that the five governments are going to try to dictate to, or dominate, other nations. It will be their duty to apply, so far as possible, the fundamental principles of justice underlying the Charter adopted at San Francisco.

Just as the meeting at Dumbarton Oaks drew up the proposals to be placed before the conference at San Francisco, so this Council of Foreign Ministers will lay the groundwork for future peace settlements. This preparation by the Council will make possible speedier, more orderly, more efficient and more cooperative peace settlements than could otherwise be obtained.

One of the first tasks of the Council of Ministers is to draft proposed treaties of peace with former enemy countries—Italy, Rumania, Bulgaria, Hungary, and Finland.

These treaties, of course, will have to be passed upon by all the nations concerned. In our own country, the Senate will have to ratify them. But we shall begin at once the necessary preparatory work. Adequate study now may avoid the planting of the seeds of future wars.

I am sure that the American people will agree with me that this Council of Foreign Ministers will be effective in hastening the day of peace and reconstruction.

We were anxious to settle the future of Italy first among the former enemy countries. Italy was the first to break away from the Axis.

She helped materially in the final defeat of Germany. She has now joined us in the war against Japan. She is making real progress toward democracy.

A peace treaty with a democratic Italian Government will make it possible for us to receive Italy as a member of the United Nations.

The Council of Foreign Ministers will also have to start the preparatory work for the German peace settlement. But its final acceptance will have to wait until Germany has developed a government with which a peace treaty can be made. In the meantime, the conference of Berlin laid down the specific political and economic principles under which Germany will be governed by the occupying powers.

.   .   .   .

We are going to do what we can to make Germany over into a decent nation, so that it may eventually work its way from the economic chaos it has brought upon itself, back into a place in the civilized world.

.   .   .   .

One of the persistent causes for wars in Europe in the last two centuries has been the selfish control of the waterways of Europe. I mean the Danube, the Black Sea Straits, the Rhine, the Kiel Canal, and all the inland waterways of Europe which border on two or more states.

The United States proposed at Berlin that there be free and unrestricted navigation of these inland waterways. We think this is important to the future peace and security of the world. We proposed that regulations for such navigation be provided by international authorities.

The function of the agencies would be to develop the use of the waterways and assure equal treatment on them for all nations. Membership on the agencies would include the United States, Great Britain, the Soviet Union, and France, plus those states which border on the waterways.

Our proposal was considered by the Conference and was referred to the Council of Ministers. There, the United States intends to press for its adoption.

.   .   .   .

Our victory in Europe was more than a victory of arms.

It was a victory of one way of life over another. It was a victory of an ideal founded on the rights of the common man, on the dignity of the human being, and on the conception of the state as the servant— not the master—of its people.

A free people showed that it was able to defeat professional soldiers whose only moral arms were obedience and worship of force.

We tell ourselves that we have emerged from this war the most powerful nation in the world—the most powerful nation, perhaps, in all history. That is true, but not in the sense some of us believe it to be true.

The war has shown us that we have tremendous resources to make all the materials for war. It has shown us that we have skilful workers and managers and able generals, and a brave people capable of bearing arms.

All these things we knew before.

The new thing—the thing we had not known—the thing we have learned now and should never forget, is this: that a society of self-governing men is more powerful, more enduring, more creative than any other kind of society, however disciplined, however centralized.

We know now that the basic proposition of the worth and dignity of man is not a sentimental aspiration or a vain hope or a piece of rhetoric. It is the strongest, the most creative force now present in this world.

Now let us use that force and all our resources and all our skills in the great cause of a just and lasting peace!

The three great powers are now more closely than ever bound together in determination to achieve that kind of peace. From Tehran, and the Crimea, and San Francisco, and Berlin—we shall continue to march together to our objective.

APPENDIX 2

First Session of the Council of Foreign Ministers at London, Report by James F. Byrnes, Secretary of State, October 5, 1945

THE FIRST SESSION of the Council of Foreign Ministers closed in a stalemate. But that need not, and should not, deprive us of a second and better chance to get on with the peace.

In the past I have been both criticized and commended for being a compromiser. I confess that I do believe that peace and political progress in international affairs as in domestic affairs depend upon intelligent compromise. The United States Delegation acted in that spirit at Berlin. We acted in that spirit at London. And we shall continue to act in that spirit at future conferences.

That spirit is essential in international conferences where action can be taken only by unanimous agreement. When any one member can prevent agreement, compromise is a necessity. Men and women who have served on a jury can appreciate that.

Compromise, however, does not mean surrender, and compromise unlike surrender requires the assent of more than one party.

The difficulties encountered at the London conference will, I hope, impress upon the peoples of all countries, including our own people, the hard reality that none of us can expect to write the peace in our own way. If this hard reality is accepted by statesmen and peoples at an early stage of the peace-making process, it may at later stages save us and save the peace of the world from the disastrous effects of disillusionment and intransigences.

Regardless of how Americans may differ as to domestic policies, they desire unity in our foreign policies. This unity will be essential in the days ahead of us when we may expect differences in views by various governments as to peace settlements. However, the political party in power cannot expect this unity unless it freely consults representatives of the opposing political party.

Believing this, I requested Mr. John Foster Dulles, one of the best-informed Americans in the field of foreign relations and a loyal Republican, to accompany me to London in an advisory capacity. He has been more than an adviser; he has been a partner. Between us there have been no secrets. At the Council table and in private conference he has participated in the making of all decisions. Our accord serves to show that in foreign affairs Republicans and Democrats can work together and that in vital matters of foreign policy we Americans are united.

When it was agreed at Berlin to establish the Council of Foreign Ministers I think we all had in mind the precedent of the Dumbarton Oaks conference. There, representatives of Great Britain, the Soviet Union, China, and the United States worked together to prepare draft proposals for the United Nations Charter as a basis for discussion with other nations. France was not present at Dumbarton Oaks only because France had not yet been liberated. Her right to permanent membership on the United Nations Security Council was not questioned.

Experience reveals that a certain degree of understanding among the major powers is essential to secure general agreement among many nations. When understanding among the great powers is not achieved in advance of a conference participated in by many nations, it usually has to be secured informally during the conference.

At the Versailles conference, for example, it took the Big Three and the Big Five so long to agree among themselves that the complaint was made that the smaller powers had little more time to consider the treaty than was given to the Germans.

The Berlin agreement envisaged the naming of high-ranking deputies who could carry on the work of the Council in the absence of their chiefs, the Foreign Secretaries. The Council, as President Truman and I understood it, was to be a sort of combined staff to explore the problems and prepare proposals for the final peace settlements.

At Berlin it certainly was never intended that the three powers present or the five powers constituting the Council should take unto themselves the making of the final peace. The Berlin declaration setting up the Council begins with the statement, "The Conference reached the following agreement for the establishment of a Council of Foreign Ministers to do the necessary preparatory work for the peace settlements."

The Council was not to make the peace settlements but to do the necessary preparatory work for the peace settlements. It certainly was not my intention to agree to any final treaty without first getting the views of the Foreign Relations Committee of the Senate which must pass upon all treaties before ratification.

The first session of the Council, so far as the personal participation of the Foreign Ministers was concerned, was intended to provide directives for the deputies in the preparation of treaties for Italy, Rumania, Bulgaria, Hungary, and Finland.

This work was exploratory—to find out on what points we were in agreement, on what points we differed, and on what points further study and data were required. It is a little naive to suppose that when really vital differences emerge, one nation or another is likely to abandon its position on the first interchange of views.

At this stage it is as important to know and understand wherein we and our Allies differ as wherein we agree. We must understand our points of difference before we can intelligently consider means of reconciling them.

So far as the Italian treaty was concerned I think we made very good progress toward agreement on directives to govern the work of our deputies.

There was ready acceptance of our proposal that Italy should undertake to maintain a bill of rights which will secure the freedoms of speech, religious worship, political belief and public meeting envisaged for Italy in the Moscow Declaration of November 1943 and which will confirm the human rights and fundamental freedoms set forth in the Charter of the United Nations.

There was some difference among the conferees at the start as to providing for the limitation of armaments. But it was our feeling that Italy should rely on the United Nations for protection against aggression and should not engage in competition in armaments when all her resources are badly needed to restore her civilian economy. And this view gained general acceptance.

While the very controversial boundary dispute between Yugoslavia and Italy was not settled, it was encouraging to find that it was possible to agree that the line should in the main be governed by ethnic considerations and that regardless of its sovereignty there should be a free port at Trieste under international control.

The Council was in general agreement that the Dodecanese Islands should go to Greece although the assent of one member was qualified pending the study of certain questions by his government.

There was general agreement that the Italian colonies should come under the trusteeship provisions of the United Nations Charter. Various views were expressed as to the preferred form of trusteeship for the colonies.

The American Delegation was particularly gratified that the directive to the deputies, while not restricting their studies, called for special consideration of the American proposal for a truly international administration directly responsible to the United Nations with a view to the attainment of the greatest degree of independence of the inhabitants of two of the colonies at the end of ten years and independence for the people of a third colony at as early a date as possible.

This proposal was presented by the American Delegation when the Italian treaty first was taken up and was consistently adhered to.

It is our view that the object of a trusteeship should be to promote the self-government of the people of a colony and not to enrich a trustee or increase its economic or military power.

It was also agreed that Italian sovereignty should be restored on the conclusion of the treaty so that foreign troops may be withdrawn and, except as specially provided in the treaty, foreign controls within Italy terminated.

There was no definite understanding on reparations. The United States took the position that Italy could not pay anything like $600,000,000. Apart from certain foreign assets, she should be required to pay as reparations only such factory and tool equipment designed for the manufacture of war implements which are not required for the limited military establishment permitted to her and which cannot be readily converted to peaceful purposes. If she is stripped of more, then her economy cannot be restored.

We have contributed several hundred million dollars for the relief of the Italian people. Their condition is deplorable. We must continue to help them. But we cannot contribute more millions, if those millions are to be used to enable Italy to pay reparations to other governments. We did that for Germany after the last war. We shall not do it again.

Substantial progress was also made on the directives for the preparatory work on the Finnish treaty and the treaties with Rumania and Bulgaria. The principles suggested by the American Delegation and accepted for the Italian treaty for the safeguarding of human rights and fundamental freedoms are also to be incorporated in these treaties.

The directives concerning the limitation of armament for Rumania and Bulgaria are expected to follow the same general line as those accepted for Italy.

Before work could be commenced upon the directives for the Hungarian treaty the Soviet Delegation announced they felt obliged to withdraw their assent to the procedure previously accepted by the Council for dealing with peace treaties.

Before taking up these procedural difficulties I should say a few words about the Soviet Delegation's disappointment with the failure of Great Britain and the United States to recognize the Bulgarian and Rumanian Governments.

The thought apparently exists in their mind that our government objects to these governments because they are friendly to the Soviet

Union and that our unwillingness to recognize these governments is a manifestation of unfriendliness to the Soviet Union.

There could be no greater misconception of our attitude. I was at Yalta. The Yalta declaration on the liberated and ex-satellite countries was based on a proposal submitted by President Roosevelt. Under it the Allied Powers, including the Soviet Union, assumed the responsibility of concerting their policies to assist in the establishment of interim governments broadly representative of all important democratic elements in the population and pledged to the earliest possible establishment through free elections of governments responsive to the will of the people. That pledge cannot be fulfilled in countries where freedom of speech and of assembly are denied.

That policy sponsored by President Roosevelt was America's policy and remains America's policy.

We are well aware that no government is perfect and that the representative character of any provisional government will always be subject to debate. We do not demand perfection where perfection is unobtainable.

In an effort to concert our policies with our Allies we have tried to show a spirit of conciliation. Certainly we did not make unduly exacting the requirements we set before we recognized the Provisional Polish Government or the conditions which we have proposed as a basis for the recognition of the Provisional Hungarian Government.

And I hope that as the result of efforts now being made by the Provisional Austrian Government to broaden its representation, we may soon be able to recognize that Government.

At Berlin we stated we would examine in the near future, in the light of prevailing conditions, the question of recognition of Rumania and Bulgaria. We have investigated and we shall continue to investigate. But we cannot know whether conditions justify recognition unless our political representatives are fully informed and unless our news correspondents are permitted freely to enter countries and freely to send their stories uncensored.

We do not seek to dictate the internal affairs of any people. We only reserve for ourselves the right to refuse to recognize governments if after investigation we conclude they have not given to the people the rights pledged to them in the Yalta agreement and in the Atlantic Charter.

The peace of Europe depends upon the existence of friendly relations between the Soviet Union and its European neighbors, and two wars in one generation have convinced the American people that they have a very vital interest in the maintenance of peace in Europe.

The American Government shares the desire of the Soviet Union to have governments friendly to the Soviet Union in eastern and central Europe.

But lasting peace depends not only upon friendship between governments but upon friendship between peoples.

Had it not been for the difficulties experienced by the Allied Governments in agreeing upon a common policy in regard to the recognition of the Governments of Rumania and Bulgaria a more conciliatory spirit might possibly have prevailed and might greatly have helped to overcome the procedural difficulties of the Council.

No one present at the Council on September 11 questioned the decision taken by the Council that day inviting all five members to be present at all meetings.

Directives for the Italian treaty were under discussion for several days with China, not a party to the surrender terms, present, participating in the discussion, but not voting. No one objected.

Directives for the Finnish treaty were then considered, with the United States, France, and China present but not voting. No one objected.

Directives for the Rumanian treaty and then for the Bulgarian treaty were considered, with France and China present but not voting. No one objected.

It was only on September 22 that the Soviet Delegation took the position that the decision of the Council on September 11 violated the Berlin agreement.

It will be recalled that the Berlin agreement set up a Council of the Soviet Union, Great Britain, France, China and the United States to undertake the necessary preparatory work for the peace settlements. It provided that the Council should draw up with a view to their submission to the United Nations peace treaties with Italy, Rumania, Bulgaria, Hungary, and Finland.

It provided that in the discharge of these tasks the Council will be composed of members representing those states which were signatory to the terms of surrender imposed upon the enemy state concerned, and for the purpose of the Italian settlement, France should be regarded as signatory to the surrender terms.

The Berlin agreement further provided that other members of the Council will be invited to participate when matters directly concerning them are under discussion.

This distinction between members of the Council who were parties to the surrender terms and those who were not, was not part of the original American proposal and was reluctantly accepted by us. We were fully aware that a member would not have the right to vote if not a party to the surrender terms, but we understood from the exchange of views at the table that all members would be allowed to participate in all discussions in the Council.

It certainly never occurred to President Truman or myself that any of the five members of the Council who are also the five permanent members of the United Nations Security Council, which is charged with the responsibility for maintaining the peace which the Council of Foreign Ministers is preparing, would not be invited to be present during the discussions of the treaties.

Such exclusion of two permanent members of the Security Council would not promote the harmonious relations essential to the success of the United Nations Organization.

The Soviet Delegation's position was not simply that they wished to withdraw the invitation to China and France to participate without right to vote. Their position was that it was beyond the authority of the states signatory to the surrender terms to extend the invitation.

Although this construction of the Berlin agreement did not accord with the understanding of the American Delegation or the British Delegation or the President of the United States or the Prime Minister of Great Britain, the Soviet Delegation insisted that they could no longer discuss treaty matters in the presence of members who were not parties to the surrender terms.

Thereafter the meetings of the Council for a number of days were confined to the discussion of other items on the agenda such as international inland waterways, the Ruhr, acceleration of German reparations, restitution, repatriation of Allied nationals, and the Austrian food supply.

When the general items on the agenda were exhausted, agreement had not been reached for solving the procedural obstacles which, in the view of the Soviet Delegation, made further discussion of treaty matters impossible until the decision of September 11 should be rescinded.

Since it had always been my view that the Berlin agreement contemplated a broadening out of the participants before the final conclusion of a peace treaty, I sought to find a compromise along that line.

The Berlin agreement expressly provided in section 4 of the article establishing the Council that the Council may adapt its procedures to the particular problems under discussion; that in some cases it may hold its own discussions prior to the participation of other interested states; and in other cases it may convoke a formal conference of states interested in particular problems.

I therefore proposed, with considerable reluctance, that we ask our French and Chinese colleagues to accept the position of the Soviet

Delegation that the preparatory and exploratory work of the Council for the peace settlements be confined to the signatories of the surrender terms in question, provided that at the same time it should be agreed that a truly representative peace conference should be convoked before the end of the year. To ensure the calling of such a conference we thought that France and China, in the interest of peace, might make even this sacrifice.

This conference would be convoked for the purpose of considering the peace treaties with Italy, Rumania, Bulgaria, Hungary, and Finland. To the conference would be invited—

(1) The five members of the Council of Foreign Ministers which are also the five permanent members of the United Nations Security Council;

(2) All European members of the United Nations;

(3) All non-European members of the United Nations which supplied substantial military contingents in the war against the European members of the Axis.

The American Delegation took the position that, in an interdependent, democratic world, peace cannot be the exclusive concern of a few presently powerful states; that unless we were to revert to a world of isolationism none of the states which we wanted invited to the peace conference could be said to be not directly concerned in the peace.

We urged that those states, both large and small, which had fought and suffered in the war must make the peace. This has been a peoples' war and it must be a peoples' peace.

The Soviet Delegation stated, however, that they could not agree to the American proposal for a peace conference until they had returned to Moscow and had personal consultations with their Government.

It therefore became obvious that there could be no agreement unless the other delegations were prepared to yield their views and convictions to those of the Soviet Delegation. This none of the other delegations was prepared to do.

The United States is willing to dictate terms of peace to an enemy but it is not willing to dictate terms of peace to its Allies.

Our task then became one of arranging an adjournment until the Soviet Delegation could return to Moscow. It is customary before adjournment to adopt and have all conferees to sign a protocol containing a record of the agreed decisions of a conference. The Soviet Delegation would not agree to the inclusion in the protocol of the decision of September 11 that the five members should participate in all meetings, even though it included a statement of the action taken by the Soviet Delegation on September 22 to withdraw their assent to that decision.

On the last day of the session the Soviet Delegation announced it would offer a compromise proposal. The proposal was that there should be four separate protocols without recording in any of them the decision of September 11 which had been agreed to by them but which they later wished to rescind. This was the same position that they had urged for days. The only thing new about it was the suggestion that on the following day they would discuss unsettled questions including the American proposal for a peace conference and the disputed September 11 decision.

In answer to a question the Soviet Foreign Minister stated that while he could discuss the proposal for a peace conference, he still was without authority to act upon it. The proposal had been discussed for a week. Further discussion without action was futile.

It was also obvious that once the four protocols were signed, it would be useless on the following day to discuss the question of inserting in the protocols the decision of September 11. An objection by the Soviet Delegation would prevent its insertion.

The Soviet Delegation also reiterated their position that they would not discuss the treaties in the presence of members they now believed to be ineligible. This would have excluded China from the consideration of all treaties and France from the consideration of all but one without any assurance of participation in a peace conference.

It became apparent that agreement was impossible and further meetings were useless. The Chinese Foreign Minister who was presiding when the Council adjourned and at whose instance the Council had remained in session from Sunday until Tuesday, stated that under the circumstances he could not ask the Council to continue in session longer.

As the record stands the Foreign Minister of the Soviet Union has not rejected our proposal for a peace conference. During the discussions he admitted it was correct in principle. My hope is that, after he has conferred with his government, his government will agree that the nations that fought the war—the World War—shall have a chance to make the world peace.

The matter that caused the suspension of our work is no trivial or technical question. It presented an issue that had to be met. It is whether the peace shall be made by three or even five nations to the exclusion of other nations vitally concerned in the maintenance and enforcement of the peace which is being prepared.

The issue goes even deeper. The Council of Foreign Ministers acts under the unanimity rule just as the Security Council of the United Nations must act in many important matters, but in the Security

Council no nation has the veto power in procedural matters while in the Council of Foreign Ministers one nation can veto all action.

The veto power is a great power and should not be lightly exercised. We are willing to make many concessions but the United States does not believe in agreement at any price.

The power of veto in procedural matters should not be used by the United States or any other nation to coerce the judgment and conscience of fellow nations.

Peace must be based upon mutual understanding and mutual respect. It can not be secured by procedural maneuverings which obscure from the people the real and vital issues upon which their peace depends.

Undeterred by temporary set-backs and ever willing to accord to others that tolerant understanding that we wish others to accord to us, we must not relax in our efforts to achieve a just and lasting peace for ourselves and all nations. "With firmness in the right as God gives us to see the right, let us strive on to finish the work we are in."

APPENDIX 3

Moscow Meeting of Foreign Ministers, December 16–26, 1945, Report by James F. Byrnes, Secretary of State

THE PURPOSE of my talk tonight is to render a report on the recent meeting of the Foreign Secretaries of Great Britain, the United States, and the Soviet Union at Moscow.

With President Truman's approval and encouragement I had urged the calling of this meeting in fulfilment of the understanding reached at Yalta that the three Foreign Secretaries should meet every three or four months.

I was well aware of the risk involved in suggesting this meeting without any definite assurance that the three governments would be able to reach agreement on the points under discussion. I knew the risk of another impasse such as occurred in London. I felt this risk had to be taken.

It is just when there are genuine difficulties in reaching agreement that Foreign Secretaries should meet in an effort to understand each other's problems and troubles.

In this modern world where events move with lightning speed there is not time to wait for agreement to be reached by the slow exchange of diplomatic communications.

We must realize that discussion and personal contact in international affairs are useful and helpful even though they do not at once lead to agreement. They contribute to a meeting of the minds and the reconciliation of differences.

In September the Council of Foreign Ministers at London had been unable to agree upon the procedure to be followed in drawing up the European peace treaties. The Soviet Union took the position that the treaties should be made only by the principal powers who had signed the respective armistices. The other delegations took the view that all states which took an active part in the war should be allowed to participate in the peace.

While we could not agree at London, and many referred to the London conference as a complete failure, it was, I think, the discussions at London that helped us greatly to reach agreement on peace machinery at Moscow.

The agreement at Moscow meets our insistence that all states which took an active part in the war should participate in the peace. It also frankly recognizes the responsible role of the larger powers in the making of peace.

Our agreement is that the terms of peace in the first instance should be drawn by the principal powers which were signers of the respective armistices. But it was decided that as soon as these terms were drawn up, they should be submitted to a peace conference called by the five states—the United States, the Soviet Union, Great Britain, France, and China, who constitute the Council of Foreign Ministers and are the permanent members of the Security Council of the United Nations. All states which actively waged war with substantial military force against the European members of the Axis will be invited to participate in the conference.

The peace conference is to be called not later than May 1.

The conference will consider the draft treaties prepared by the states that signed the respective armistices. The peace conference will then draw up its own recommendations. After that, the states which prepared the preliminary texts will consider the recommendations of the peace conference and prepare the final texts of the treaties to be signed by all states actively at war with the enemy states in question.

I do not consider this solution ideal. But the departure from the ideal standard is more in the form than the substance. What is preserved is that the proposals of the larger powers are subjected to the judgment and public criticism of all the nations which took an active part in the war. The procedure contemplates and requires that these nations formally and publicly make their recommendations. The larger powers are not bound by these recommendations, but they must agree in order to draw up the final treaties. Certainly the United States would not agree to a final treaty which arbitrarily rejected such recommendations. Certainly the great powers which drew up the draft charter for the United Nations at Dumbarton Oaks did not ignore the changes suggested by the smaller powers at San Francisco.

The test of a successful peace is not in the form of its making, but whether it both commends itself to the nations concerned by its justice and wisdom and also commands the support of those nations whose unity is essential to preserve the peace. The method agreed upon at Moscow gives ample scope for the achievement of these essential results.

The question of the recognition of the ex-satellite states was discussed. Since the London conference, we have found it possible to recognize Austria and Hungary where free elections have occurred.

There is still a wide divergence in our viewpoints on the Governments of Rumania and Bulgaria. That divergence is accentuated by the fact that in those countries democratic institutions have not functioned in accordance with traditions familiar to us.

The Soviet Union contends that the governments of those countries are satisfactory and conditions do not warrant concerted action under the Yalta Agreement. And concerted action is possible only by common agreement.

Our objections to the Rumanian and Bulgarian Governments have been not only to the exclusion of important democratic groups from those governments, but to the oppressive way in which those governments exercise their powers. Until now our objections have been little heeded by those governments or by the Soviet Government.

It must be recognized that the Soviet Government has a very real interest in the character of the governments of these states. These countries are neighbors of the Soviet Union and were involved in the war against the Soviet Union. It is therefore to be expected that the withdrawal of Soviet troops from these countries may depend upon the Soviet Government's confidence in the peaceful character of these governments.

I urged upon Generalissimo Stalin and Foreign Minister Molotov that it was in their interest as well as ours, that the peoples of these countries, as well as their governments, should be peacefully disposed toward the Soviet Union. I stressed the fact that it was our desire to work with the Soviet Government and not against it in making these governments more representative. And for the first time since Yalta the Soviet Government has agreed to cooperate with us to this end.

A tripartite commission is to proceed immediately to Rumania to advise the King, who has sought the advice of the three Allied governments, on broadening representation in the Rumanian Government. At London we asked this but were unable to secure agreement.

The British and American Governments have agreed that they will recognize the Rumanian Government as soon as they are satisfied that the Government has been broadened to include two truly representative members of two important political parties not now represented in the Government and assurances have been given regarding free elections, freedom of speech, press, religion, and association. These are the terms under which we will recognize this government. It is for us to say whether the terms have been complied with.

The situation in Bulgaria is complicated by the fact that an election has already occurred there which the Soviet Government regards as a free election and we do not. Nevertheless, the Soviet Government has undertaken to advise the new Bulgarian Government to include in the government two members truly representative of important political parties not now included. The British Government and the American Government have stated that as soon as they are satisfied that this has been done they will recognize the new Bulgarian Government.

The agreements regarding Rumania and Bulgaria do not go as far as I should have liked, but I am hopeful that they will result in a substantial improvement in the democratic character of these governments.

In the Far East, it has been our policy to work for the creation of conditions that make for lasting peace. Cooperation with our Allies is an essential part of that policy.

While the United States sustained the major burden in crushing the military power of Japan, we have always considered the war against Japan a part of the war against the Axis. From the outset we have planned to make the control of Japan an Allied responsibility.

As early as August 20 we invited the Soviet Union, Great Britain, and China to join with us in carrying out the objectives of the Potsdam Declaration and the Terms of Surrender for Japan. The Far Eastern Advisory Commission was established in October, but Great Britain had reservations regarding its advisory character, and the Soviet Union requested a decision regarding control machinery in Tokyo before joining the work of the Commission.

At Moscow the three Governments, with the concurrence of China, agreed on a Far Eastern Commission. It will consist of representatives of the Soviet Union, Great Britain, China, the United States, France, Netherlands, Australia, New Zealand, Canada, India, and the Philippines.

This Far Eastern Commission will have the authority to formulate principles to govern the control of Japan. It will act by a majority vote which, however, must include the concurring votes of Great Britain, the Soviet Union, China, and the United States. The decisions of the Commission will be incorporated into directives to the Supreme Commander by the United States Government.

Under the agreement establishing the Commission no basic allied policy for Japan may be adopted without our concurrence.

Pending agreement in the Far Eastern Commission in case of need we are free to give interim directives on all urgent matters. Only three questions are excepted from our authority to give interim directives. The questions reserved for action by the Commission—which action requires our concurrence—are questions dealing with changes in the control of Japan as set forth in the surrender terms or with fundamental changes in the Japanese constitutional structure or with changes in the Japanese Government as a whole.

These are questions which by their nature require agreement among the principal allies if there is to be a common allied policy. To reserve them for decision by the Commission does not affect the administration of allied control by the Supreme Commander.

It has not been our policy to dictate changes in the Japanese Government as a whole, and so far as it is necessary to make individual changes in the cabinet or to fill vacancies created by the resignation of individual members the authority of the Supreme Commander to act remains unimpaired.

The three Governments also agreed, with the concurrence of China, on the establishment of an Allied Council for Japan to be composed of representatives of the Soviet Union, the British Commonwealth, China, and the United States under the chairmanship of General MacArthur as the Supreme Allied Commander. The Council is to advise and consult with the Supreme Commander in carrying out the Terms of Surrender. His decision will be controlling on all but the three reserved questions I have just mentioned.

If any disagreement arises in the Council regarding the implementation of a policy decision of the Far Eastern Commission upon any of these three points, the Supreme Commander will withhold action pending a clarification of its decision by the Far Eastern Commission. But when necessary, as I have already explained, the Supreme Commander, after appropriate consultation with the Council, may change individual ministers or fill vacancies.

The proposals we offered regarding Japan make it clear that we intend to cooperate with our Allies and we expect them to cooperate with us. But at the same time our agreement safeguards the efficient administration which has been set up in Japan under the Supreme Allied Commander.

It assures that the authority of General MacArthur will not be obstructed by the inability of the Far Eastern Commission to agree on policies or by the inability of the Allied Council to agree upon the methods of carrying them out.

We were determined to assure that the outstanding and efficient administration set up and executed by General MacArthur should not be obstructed.

The administration of Korea has been a trying problem since the surrender of Japan. For purposes of military operations the occupation of Korea was divided north and south of latitude 38 into Soviet and American areas. The continuation of this division after surrender has been unsatisfactory. The movement of persons and goods and the functioning of public services on a nationwide scale has been hampered.

Under our agreement at Moscow, the two military commands are to form a joint Soviet-American Commission to solve immediate economic and administrative problems. They will make recommendations to the Governments of the United States, the Soviet Union, Great Britain, and China for the formation of a Korean provisional democratic government. They will also make proposals to these governments regarding a four-power trusteeship to prepare Korea for its independence within five years.

The joint Soviet-American Commission, working with the Korean provisional democratic government, may find it possible to dispense with a trusteeship. It is our goal to hasten the day when Korea will become an independent member of the society of nations.

In the various agreements and understandings reached in Moscow the interests of China were taken into full account. China is to participate in the Council of Foreign Ministers, the Far Eastern Commission, in the four-power Allied Council in Tokyo, in the formation of a Korean provisional national government, and in any trusteeship for Korea.

But China divided by civil strife will not be able to take its rightful place among its Allies and discharge properly its international responsibilities.

Our policy toward China as recently announced by President Truman was discussed at Moscow. We found our Allies in substantial accord with that policy. The three Governments agreed that the cessation of civil strife and broad participation throughout the National Government of democratic elements are necessary to assure a unified, peaceful, and democratic China under the National Government. The three Governments reaffirmed adherence to the policy of non-interference in the internal affairs of China.

Mr. Molotov and I discussed the problem of Soviet and American armed forces in China. The Soviet Union, pursuant to their agreement with the National Government of China, plans to remove its forces from Manchuria by February 1st. We will move our Marines from north China when Japanese troops are disarmed and deported from China or when China is able to complete the task unassisted by us.

The understanding of the three Powers as to policy toward China should assist General Marshall in the mission he has undertaken.

The British and ourselves came to Moscow with a very definite proposal for the establishment by the United Nations of a commission on atomic energy and related matters based on the Washington declaration of the President of the United States and the Prime Ministers of Great Britain and Canada on that subject. At the request of the Soviet Government the discussion of our proposal was placed at the end of our agenda. Our discussions were limited to this proposal. At no time did we discuss any technical or scientific matters, nor were we asked by the Soviet Government about the new weapon. I was happy to find that the Soviet Government feels as we do that this particular weapon is of such a revolutionary nature that we should explore through a United Nations commission methods of international control.

It should be understood that the task of the commission is to inquire into the problems raised by the discovery of atomic energy and related matters and to make recommendations. Neither the Security Council nor the commission has authority to bind any government to act on its recommendations.

The four objectives set forth in the proposed resolution establishing the commission are not intended to indicate the order in which they are to be considered. In particular, it was intended and is understood that the matter of safeguards will apply to the recommendations of the commission in relation to every phase of the subject and at every stage. Indeed, at the root of the whole matter lies the problem of providing the necessary safeguards.

Neither we nor any other nation would be expected to share our armament secrets until it was certain that effective safeguards had been developed to insure our mutual protection.

The Soviet Government offered only a few amendments to the proposal submitted by us. These amendments were designed to clarify the relations of the commission to the Security Council. With some revisions we accepted them.

Carefully examined, these amendments will be found to go no further than appropriate to enable the Security Council to exercise its primary responsibility for the maintenance of peace and security.

The Security Council can give directions to the commission and restrain publication of reports detrimental to peace and security, but such action can be taken only with the concurrence of all its permanent members. Failure of the Security Council to act cannot block the work of the commission.

The three Governments have invited France, China, and Canada to join with us in submitting the proposed resolution to the Assembly of the United Nations.

The Foreign Ministers reached understanding on all important items placed on our agenda with the exception of Iran. At one time it looked as if we might agree on a tripartite commission to consider Iranian problems which have been accentuated by the presence of Allied troops in Iran. Unfortunately, we could not agree. I do not wish to minimize the seriousness of the problem. But I am not discouraged. I hope that the exchange of views may lead to further consideration of the grave issues involved and out of such consideration a solution may be found.

There was no subject as to which an agreement was reached that was not covered in the communiqué published Friday, apart from instructions to the representatives of the three Governments to facilitate agreements in the field.

The agreements reached should bring hope to the war-weary people of many lands. They will facilitate the signing of peace treaties which is necessary to permit the withdrawal of troops from occupied territories. Only by the withdrawal of armies of occupation can the people have an opportunity to start on the long road to economic recovery. Only by economic recovery of other countries can we in America hope for the full employment of our labor and our capital in this interdependent world.

We must realize that international conferences are not intended to give individual statesmen the opportunity to achieve diplomatic successes. They are intended to be useful in the adjustment of delicate social and human relations between states with many common interests and many divergent interests.

In international affairs, as in national affairs, conflicting interests can be reconciled only by frank discussion and better understanding. The meeting in Moscow did serve to bring about better understanding. We must not slacken in our efforts. With patience, good will, and tolerance we must strive to build and maintain a just and enduring peace.

APPENDIX 4

First Part of the Paris Meeting of Foreign Ministers, Report by James F. Byrnes, Secretary of State, May 20, 1946

I wish to talk with you about the meeting of the Council of Foreign Ministers at Paris. On this mission I was accompanied by Senator Connally, Chairman of the Senate Foreign Relations Committee, and Senator Vandenberg, a Republican member of that Committee. I cannot adequately express my appreciation of their wise counsel and loyal cooperation. Senator Connally was exceedingly helpful. Senator Vandenberg by his wholehearted cooperation let the world know that regardless of how much he and his party may disagree with the administration about domestic issues, in our relations with foreign governments we have but one policy, the policy of the United States.

Building the foundations of a people's peace in a war-shattered world is a long, hard process. A people's peace cannot be won by flashing diplomatic triumphs. It requires patience and firmness, tolerance and understanding. We must not try to impose our will on others, but we must make sure that others do not get the impression they can impose their will on us.

The progress made towards peace at the Paris meeting of the Council of Foreign Ministers was disappointingly small in light of the expectations we had when it was agreed at Moscow last December that the Council should resume the work which had been interrupted by our inability to agree at London last September.

But the progress towards peace at Paris was infinitely greater than I expected when I suggested that the Council should meet in Paris preparatory to the prompt calling of a peace conference. The Ministers did come to Paris seriously intending to pave the way for a peace conference. We differed considerably on a number of fundamental points; but we did come to know what those fundamental points were and the varying weight the different Ministers attached to those points.

We found that there were three basic issues outstanding on the Italian treaty: reparations, the colonies and the Italian-Yugoslav boundary, particularly as it concerns the Italian city of Trieste.

In summarizing the significance of these basic issues, I shall deliberately seek to avoid intensifying the conflict in viewpoints.

Our position on reparations is simple. To enable the Italian nation to live we have already advanced directly or indirectly $900,000,000. We should prefer in the interest of peace to forget about reparations. But we are willing to agree to limited reparations, provided these do not deprive Italy of resources necessary to enable her to subsist without external assistance.

If Italy requires help from others she will look to us. And we made it clear we are not going to advance millions of dollars to enable Italy to produce goods to be paid as reparations to any of our Allies.

The Soviet Government has insisted on reparations for itself of $100,000,000. We have pointed out certain sources from which reparations can be taken which would not seriously affect the Italian economy and which would yield substantially the amount which the Soviets claim. But the Soviet Government is unwilling to count what she will obtain from some of these sources as reparations.

For example, she insists that some of the naval ships surrendered by Italy to the navies of the United States and Britain be shared with her. She declares the ships are war booty. But war booty belongs to the nation capturing it. The Soviet Union has never shared with Allied nations any war booty captured by her. We are willing to give to her in lieu of reparations some of the naval ships surrendered to us. She demands the ships but refuses to consider them as a substitute for reparations. She insists upon being paid out of current production. We would have to finance the production, and therefore I refused to agree to the proposal.

Differences regarding the colonies have been narrowed but not resolved. The Soviet Government receded from its claim for a trusteeship of Tripolitania, first in favor of a joint Soviet-Italian trusteeship and later in favor of an Italian trusteeship as originally proposed by the French.

Our position has always been that the colonies should be placed under United Nations trusteeship, having as its objective the welfare of the inhabitants and their independence at the earliest practicable date. The Trusteeship Council should appoint a neutral administrator responsible to it, thus avoiding all possible rivalry between the powers. Libya and Eritrea should be granted independence in ten years.

It is open to question whether Italy is in an economic position to assume the responsibility of trusteeship and whether the return of the colonies to Italy as trustee takes sufficiently into account the wishes of the inhabitants. For these reasons it was with considerable reluctance that I indicated my willingness to yield to the French suggestion of an Italian trusteeship if that would bring about an agreement in the Council, and if it were agreed that a definite date would be fixed for the independence of Libya and Eritrea. But the French Government was unwilling to agree to a fixed date for independence.

The British felt that because of their promises during the war they could not agree to an Italian trusteeship for territory occupied by the Senussi tribes. For security reasons they also proposed a British trusteeship for Cyrenaica.

When no agreement was reached, I again urged the original American proposal for a United Nations trusteeship.

It was my impression that agreement on reparations and the colonies as well as on a host of other questions would not be long delayed if only a solution of the Trieste problem could be found. The Soviet Representative finally indicated that there would be no serious question on the cession of the Dodecanese Islands to Greece but he refused to approve it until the other territorial dispositions could be agreed upon.

The experts appointed to investigate the Italian-Yugoslav frontier did not differ as to the facts. But the Soviet Representative differs from the other members of the Council as to the conclusions to be drawn from the facts. It is his position that Venezia Giulia must be treated as an inseparable whole, and that so treated the claim of Yugoslavia to the area is superior to that of Italy. The other Representatives believe that wise statesmanship as well as the explicit decision taken by the Council at London requires a boundary line which will in the main be an ethnic line leaving a minimum of people under alien rule.

It was wrong to give Italy the whole of Venezia Giulia after World War I. It would be equally wrong to give Yugoslavia the whole of Venezia Giulia now. It would transfer from Italy to Yugoslavia approximately 500,000 Italians.

The British and French experts proposed ethnic lines more favorable to Yugoslavia than our own. In an effort to reach agreement we stated we were willing to accept the British or French line or any other ethnic line that could be justified upon the basis of the London decision.

The American Delegation suggested a plebiscite for the area between the line proposed by the United States and the line proposed by the Soviet Union—but the Soviet Delegation would not consider a plebiscite except for the whole Venezia Giulia area. All of us are agreed that

Yugoslavia and the countries of Central Europe which have for years used the port of Trieste shall have free access to Trieste at which there shall be a free port under international control. But we will continue to appeal to the Soviet Government and the Yugoslav Government not to press for a boundary line which will needlessly violate ethnic principles and will breed trouble in the future.

Agreement on the Balkan treaties is blocked principally by the inability of the Council to agree upon the economic clauses. Agreement on these provisions may have been delayed as part of a bargaining process, although so far the Soviet Government has stood out against the inclusion in the treaties of any provision which would promise freedom of commerce on the Danube, the gateway to Central Europe.

If the Soviet Government is opposed, as the United States Government is opposed, to the formation of exclusive political and economic blocs, they will not persist in their refusal to permit the countries of Central Europe to open their gates to the commerce of all nations.

It is regrettable that our outstanding differences on the treaties could not have been adjusted at our recent meeting in Paris. A short recess to allow a calm re-examination of our respective positions should expedite agreement when we reconvene. But when a world short of goods and short of food is crying for the return of conditions of peace, we cannot indefinitely delay the making of peace and the withdrawal of troops from occupied areas. The four Allied governments cannot indefinitely delay the making of peace with countries which they have long ceased to fight, simply because they cannot agree among themselves on peace terms. The Council of Foreign Ministers was formed to facilitate and not obstruct the making of peace.

If a peace conference is not called this summer, the United States will feel obliged to request the General Assembly of the United Nations under Article 14 of the Charter to make recommendations with respect to the peace settlements. But I confidently expect a peace conference to be called this summer.

The situation which we will face in the coming months will be a test not only of others but of ourselves. There are now and there will be in the future many occasions which might impel us to say as we did after the last war that, much as we would like to cooperate in the restoration of Europe, cooperation as a practical matter is impossible without the sacrifice of our principles and that we must be content to cultivate and defend our own hemisphere.

But we must not forget that if we fail to cooperate in a peace which is indivisible we may again find that we will have to cooperate in a war which is world-wide. Whether we like it or not, we live in one world.

I am unwilling to admit that we cannot cooperate without sacrifice of our principles. If we are going to play our part we must take the offensive for peace as we took the offensive for war.

But the victories of peace like those of war require sacrifice not of principle but for principle. They require faith in ourselves and in our ideals. They require initiative, resourcefulness, and unrelenting effort. There is no iron curtain that the aggregate sentiments of mankind cannot penetrate.

The American Delegation at Paris did not hesitate to start the offensive for peace.

Security is the concern of every nation. But the effort of one nation to increase its security may threaten the security of other nations and cause them in turn to try to increase their own security. The quest for security may lead to less rather than more security in the world.

It is in truth extremely difficult to know to what extent the action of any nation may be ascribed to its quest for security or to its desire to expand. But some so-called security moves on the diplomatic checkerboard have not contributed to a general sense of security.

Many of these moves are said to originate in the fear of the revival of German military might.

On our way to Potsdam last summer President Truman and I discussed this situation and agreed that it should be American policy to disarm Germany and keep her disarmed and to do what we can to prevent a struggle between the powers for the control of Germany which might give Germany the chance to divide and conquer.

Those principles were stated in the Potsdam agreement. But President Truman and I thought at that time that the policy of disarming Germany and keeping Germany disarmed for a definite period of years should become a part of a solemn treaty between the principal Allied powers. Our policy should be to prevent war and not to wait until aggression gets out of hand.

It was not a new thought. It had been foreshadowed in the Moscow Declaration of 1943. Others had discussed it, but no one more forcefully than Senator Vandenberg in a speech in the Senate in January, 1945.

At the London meeting of the Council of Foreign Ministers when the Soviet Foreign Secretary seemed greatly concerned about the Soviet security requirements in the Balkans, I suggested a twenty-five year four-power treaty, to keep Germany disarmed as a means of preventing any real threat to Soviet security. I explained that we contemplated a similar joint guaranty of the disarmament of Japan.

I again proposed such a treaty in a talk with Generalissimo Stalin on December 24 while I was in Moscow. The Generalissimo said that if the United States made such a proposal he would whole-heartedly support it.

Later I also spoke to Mr. Bevin who advised me that he personally was most sympathetic to the suggestion.

In February I sent a working draft of the proposed treaty for German disarmament to the Soviet, British and the French Governments and the proposed treaty for Japanese disarmament to the Soviet, British and Chinese Governments. I invited their suggestions as to the draft.

I was informed by Mr. Bevin and M. Bidault that they favored the proposal in principle but would have a few suggestions to make. I did not hear from Mr. Molotov. Just before the Paris meeting I advised the Ministers I would like to discuss the proposal at Paris. The Soviet Minister agreed to discuss it informally but stated without specification that there were serious objections to the draft.

At Paris the Soviet Representative stated he first wanted to know if Germany was being disarmed as contemplated by the Potsdam Agreement and he feared the treaty might delay immediate disarmament. I pointed out that our proposal could not fairly be so construed; that it did not lessen the obligation to disarm Germany now but provided machinery to keep Germany disarmed.

To remove any question as to our purpose I asked General Clay to request the Allied Control Council to appoint representatives with power to go into every zone and make a report as to the disarmament of Germany.

Later the Soviet Representative stated that when Generalissimo Stalin agreed with me to support the treaty I did not have a draft of it. He said that as it could not become effective until after a German treaty was signed, consideration of it could be delayed.

It is our sincere hope that after the Soviet Union studies our proposal and comes to appreciate our earnest desire to see Germany disarmed and kept disarmed, the Soviet Union will support it wholeheartedly.

While the making of the German peace settlement may take some time, we took the initiative at Paris to propose the immediate appointment of special deputies to prepare a peace settlement which could be considered at a general Allied conference, the date of which should be fixed by the Council at its next session.

While there is no German government yet which could accept the settlement, agreement among the Allies on the nature of the settlement is necessary to enable the Allies to know the goal towards which the Allied occupation and administration should be directed and the kind of German government which should be created to accept the settlement.

I also asked that the Special Deputies on Germany be instructed to report on several pressing problems, including boundary and economic questions. We cannot, for example, continue to carry out the reparation program if Germany is not to be administered as an economic unit as agreed upon at Potsdam. Whatever boundaries are agreed upon for Germany, she must be able to subsist without external assistance. We cannot subsidize Germany to enable her to pay reparations to other nations.

I regret that the Soviet Representative was not prepared to act upon my proposal for the appointment of Special Deputies without further study. I shall renew my proposal when the Council reconvenes.

Important as the German questions are and eager as we are to press for their speedy solution, we must not and cannot delay the peace settlements with other countries. At Potsdam it was agreed that the start should be made with Italy, Bulgaria, Hungary, Rumania and Finland. While Germany must remain under occupation for some time, we cannot fail to do our part to rid the rest of Europe of the burden of the forces of occupation. There can be no recovery in Europe until we do.

It is particularly important that we press forward vigorously with the Austrian treaty. The Moscow Declaration on Austria contemplated that Austria should be regarded more as a liberated than as a satellite country. It was agreed at Potsdam that no reparations would be taken from her. She was one of the first countries in Central Europe to have free elections following the liberation. The continuance of foreign troops in Austria is an undue burden on her economy.

In February we asked that the Austrian treaty be prepared along with other treaties for satellite states. At Paris I insisted upon its preparation but the Soviet Representative declined to discuss the Austrian treaty or say when he would consider it.

The making of peace with Austria is essential to the restoration of anything like conditions of peace in Europe. As long as there is no peace with Austria and foreign troops remain on her soil, military communication lines will continue to be maintained in Rumania and Hungary and possibly Italy.

It was for that reason that the American Delegation proposed that the Council at its next meeting on June 15 should conclude as far as possible its work on the proposed drafts, but that the date for the peace conference should be definitely fixed for July 1 or July 15 and invitations should be issued at once.

It was our view that the Council had taken sufficient time to try to narrow their differences and at this stage with the principal issues defined, we should not deny to our other war partners their right to participate. The making of peace is not the exclusive prerogative of any four governments.

The Soviet Delegation insisted that invitations for the conference could not be sent until we had reconvened and agreed on all fundamental questions. Unanimous agreement was necessary and we were forced, therefore, to recess without agreement for the actual calling of the peace conference.

While the American Delegation will, when the Council reconvenes, make every effort to reach agreement on fundamental questions, it will renew its demand for the calling of a peace conference on July 1 or July 15.

If we cannot have a peace conference until the four nations agree on every subject deemed fundamental by any one of them, that will give to one member of the Council the power to stop all efforts toward peace. It would be better for the Council to submit to the peace conference a single draft of each treaty and to set forth in this draft both the matters on which agreement had been reached and those on which agreement had not been reached. This would permit free discussion in the peace conference by all the nations that did the fighting, and world opinion will then point the way to a final settlement.

If peace could be made with Austria concurrently with the treaties now under consideration, there would be no necessity or excuse for a single soldier on foreign soil in Europe with the exception of Germany and a line of communication through Poland. European States would have a chance to live and breathe.

It is American policy to press unremittingly for the conclusion of peace settlements to make possible the withdrawal of troops from countries where they do not belong and where they impose unjustified economic and social difficulties upon the people. And even without waiting for the conclusion of peace treaties it is American policy to press for the reduction of occupation troops in all countries.

Our policy of continuing to press for the return of conditions of peace, without regard to the making of formal peace treaties, finally yielded some constructive results in the case of Italy. For months we have been urging the revision of the Italian armistice so as to restore virtually complete sovereignty to Italy except in the colonies and in the controversial Venezia Giulia area. At Paris this revision was agreed to.

While the absence of a peace treaty still handicaps Italy in her effort to rebuild her broken economic and political life, the revised armistice gives the Italian Government the largest possible freedom that can be given to it without a formal peace treaty.

Our problems are serious, but I am not discouraged. Our offensive to secure peace has only begun. We are determined to work for political and economic peace in Europe, in the Near East and in the rest of the world. We shall work for it in the peace conferences and in the councils of the United Nations. The objective of our offensive is not territory or reparations for the United States. The objective is peace—not a peace founded upon vengeance or greed, but a just peace, the only peace that can endure.

APPENDIX 5

The Paris Peace Council, Report by Senator Arthur H. Vandenberg to the Senate, May 21, 1946

M R. PRESIDENT, when I returned to Washington last Saturday from Paris I had expected to address the Senate in some detail this afternoon regarding the vitally important work of the Council of Foreign Ministers which has just temporarily recessed until June 15. But when I discovered the status of the Senate calendar and the urgent necessity for earliest possible action upon pending legislation, I concluded that it would be unwise for me to divert the Senate's attention to another subject, regardless of its paramount concern to every citizen; and when Secretary of State James F. Byrnes made his able radio report to the Nation last night, it was so comprehensive and so adequate that I was confirmed in my decision to let the record stand where he left it for the time being. Therefore I content myself for the moment with this brief observation.

Secretary Byrnes requested the able chairman of the Senate Foreign Relations Committee, the Senator from Texas [Mr. Connally], and myself to accompany him to this meeting of the Council of Foreign Ministers which was summoned primarily to deal with the preparation of peace treaties with Italy, Rumania, Bulgaria, Hungary, and Finland. I am happy to say that this American delegation was a constant unit in thought and action. It had no differences. Thus, I gladly associate myself with the distinguished Secretary's report; and I compliment him upon his able leadership in this critically important enterprise.

Mr. President, the Council was not a success in gaining agreement upon several key questions upon which the solution of our major problems hangs. It did not achieve agreement on a number of controlling points. It is advisable to be entirely frank upon this score. Eastern communism and western democracy were unable, for the time being, to see eye to eye in most of these considerations.

It is unfortunate that greater progress cannot be immediately reported. But delay is preferable to error in such vital matters. We can compromise within the boundaries of a principle. We can no longer compromise principles themselves. That becomes appeasement; and appeasement only multiplies the hazard from which it seeks to escape. History leaves no room for doubt upon that score. The wrong answers will breed wars for tomorrow.

We must earnestly persist in striving for Allied unity; for unity within the principles which serve human rights and fundamental freedoms, which will win the moral judgments of the conscience of the world, and which may promise peace for "keeps". We must persist with patient firmness. We must try to understand each other. I do not despair of the results—particularly if the unselfish voice of America is a united one.

In other directions, Mr. President, the Council was at least a partial success. For example, it amended the armistice terms with Italy, once our enemy, subsequently our Ally, to permit larger native autonomy and to allow Italy more readily to recuperate as a self-sustaining member of the family of nations. It succeeded, indeed, in finding common ground in a large area of detailed actions which are involved in the mechanics of reestablished peace. Further, it succeeded in narrowing the area of dispute even in respect to the larger issues. This is progress. All these things I shall be glad to discuss in detail with the Senate at a more appropriate time.

But, in my view, Mr. President, the more important news is that the Council was a complete success in developing, at last, and in disclosing, a positive, constructive, peace-seeking bipartisan foreign policy for the United States. It is based, at last, upon the moralities of the Atlantic and the San Francisco Charters. Yet it is based equally upon the practical necessities required for Europe's rehabilitation.

It is a policy which seeks promptly to end the present inconclusive, armistice regimes which are postponing peace beyond all limits of reason and of safety. It is a policy which demands action in concluding peace treaties not only with Italy, Rumania, Bulgaria, Hungary, and Finland, but also with Austria, which is close to the center of the total, continental problem. It is a policy which demands action in arriving at decisions for a unified Germany, where the real core of Europe's recuperation resides and where the problem must be considered as a whole rather than in four airtight compartments in four zones of military occupation. It is a policy which is definite and specific upon these counts and which demands specific dead-line dates in these regards, before it is too late.

It is a policy which guarantees maximum protections against resurgent Axis aggressors, and which dramatically offers specific guaranties as an earnest of American good faith. It is a demilitarization policy. It is a policy which now substitutes justice for vengeance in these formulas of peace; which now insists upon ethnic recognitions that no longer traffic in the lives and destinies of helpless peoples; and which spurns expansionism as a plague upon tomorrow's peace and security. It is a policy which invites all of our partners in the war—instead of a closed corporation of big powers—to have a proper voice in the making of the treaties and the writing of the peace which result from the common victories which we all helped win. It is a policy which wants a people's peace.

That, Mr. President, is what I think we Americans were trying to do at Paris.

That is what I pray we may yet succeed in doing.

Mr. President, I will support that sort of a foreign policy under any administration; and I hope that any administration, whatever its political complexion, will stick to that sort of a foreign policy for keeps.

This sort of a policy, plus the effective operation of the United Nations, is the way to stop World War III before it starts.

APPENDIX 6

Text of Statement Made by James F. Byrnes, Secretary of State, on May 14, 1946, Requesting a Recess of the Council of Foreign Ministers

THE COUNCIL should frankly face the facts which it confronts. There are several minor treaty problems which require further study by our deputies or by special commissions which have them under inquiry. There is every prospect of agreement when these studies are concluded. But decisions must await this event. There are also a few major treaty problems upon which the Council is presently divided. Decisions must await further clarification and mutual study in a spirit of good will. In some instances, these decisions may be favorably affected by the reports which we await from our deputies. Our whole purpose is to seek and to find agreement as quickly as possible.

Under these circumstances, it is likely to facilitate our work if the present session of the Council recesses until June 15, permitting each of us to give undivided attention to reexamination of our positions in the hope of finding means of reconciling them. Such use of our time is calculated to be more fruitful than to extend our present session.

The American Delegation has made it clear that it believes we owe our Allied nations an obligation to fix at this time the date of a peace conference. At Moscow, we agreed it should be held not later than May 1. We did not comply with that promise. The United States now urges the peace conference be called either July 1 or July 15, and that we should then submit our agreements and our disagreements, if any, to the advice of our war partners. The Soviet representative has declined so far to agree to this course. Invitations to the Conference cannot be sent except by unanimous agreement. Therefore, the American Delegation believes the time has come to recess the Council until June 15, and, if we cannot agree on the date of the peace conference now, to commit to that session the responsibility for calling a peace conference.

Because we cannot hope for the ratification of a peace treaty with Italy for some months, we should immediately sign the revised armistice with Italy which was agreed in principle ten days ago, so as to release her recuperative efforts as far as possible.

We would urgently recommend also that Austria be put upon the June 15 agenda and our deputies instructed to prepare a draft treaty for consideration of the Council on June 15, so that it may be submitted to the Peace Conference along with the other treaties.

If we can agree to the above and if we also contemplate the wide area of agreement we have already reached, we may look to the future with confidence that our indispensable unity will be strengthened and preserved.

Therefore, the United States Delegation recommends:

First. That, after considering the German question, this session recess until June 15;

Second. That we now call a peace conference for July 1 or July 15. If this is not agreed to, that we leave to the next session of the Council the decision as to the date of the peace conference;

Third. That we immediately sign the revised armistice with Italy;

Fourth. That there be placed on the agenda for the June 15 session the drafting of a treaty with Austria, the deputies being instructed to prepare in the meantime draft proposals for the consideration of the Council.

APPENDIX 7

Latter Half of Meeting of Council of Foreign Ministers in Paris, June 15–July 12, 1946, Report by James F. Byrnes, Secretary of State

AFTER EVERY GREAT war the victors find the making of peace difficult and disappointing. It took the 13 American states more than 5 years after winning their independence to agree upon a constitution which promised anything like a durable peace among themselves.

To build world peace, bridging differences in ideas, values, codes of conduct, and deeply cherished aspirations, requires even greater tolerance, patience, and understanding. It requires the will and ability to seek *the best*, to accept the *best obtainable*, and then to make the *best obtainable* work. As war breeds war so peace can be made to breed peace.

That is why President Truman and I were determined at Potsdam last summer two months after V–E Day to set up the Council of Foreign Ministers. We were eager to have the Council start the making of peace and to make peace as quickly as possible wherever possible.

It was obvious then that the making of peace with Germany would take time. There was no German government to deal with, and no agreement as to how soon we should permit a German government to function. It was equally obvious that a start could be made toward making peace with Italy and the states which were satellites of the Axis. They had governments. So we started there.

The whole world knows how great the struggle has been during the last 10 months to harmonize the views of the great powers so as to make possible the presentation of tentative drafts of treaties to a peace conference. That struggle has now been brought to a successful conclusion and the Peace Conference has been called to meet in Paris on July 29.

In addition to the Soviet Union, the United Kingdom, France, China, and the United States, the states which are represented on the Council of Foreign Ministers, the 16 other states which took an active part in the fighting against the European Axis will be represented at the Conference.

While the Council of Foreign Ministers has made some suggestions as to the organization and procedure of the Conference, the Conference will be free to determine its own organization and procedure. It was proposed that the meetings of subcommittees should be secret. But on our objection this provision was eliminated. I gave notice that, so far as the United States is concerned, it will use its influence to open to the press the meetings of the Conference and of its committees. The Conference will make only recommendations. But the members of the Council are committed, in drafting the final texts of the treaties, to consider the recommendations of the Conference and not to reject any of them arbitrarily.

It is my hope that the Council of Foreign Ministers will consider the recommendations and agree upon the final text so that the treaties may be signed by the delegates before the Conference adjourns.

The drafts of treaties agreed upon are not the best which human wit could devise. But they are the best which human wit could get the four principal Allies to agree upon. They represent as satisfactory an approach to the return of peace as we could hope for in this imperfect and war-weary world.

The attitude of the United States in these matters represented not only the judgment of the President and the Secretary of State but also the judgment of Senator Connally and Senator Vandenberg, whose long experience in our foreign relations and intimate knowledge of the specific issues made their counsel invaluable.

The greatest struggle was over the Italian treaty, and the greatest issue involved in that treaty was the fate of Trieste and adjacent territory along the western shore of the Istrian Peninsula. The American Delegation, supported by the French and British, urged that Trieste and adjacent territory which are predominantly Italian should remain with Italy, and the predominantly Slavic hinterland should go to Yugoslavia.

The Soviet Union argued strongly that Trieste and adjacent territory should not be cut off from its immediate hinterland. While it admitted that a few cities and towns along the coast were predominantly Italian, it urged that the Istrian Peninsula should be regarded as a whole and that so regarded it was predominantly Yugoslav. This view was also urged by Czechoslovakia.

The Soviet Union further urged that greater consideration should be given to the Yugoslav claims than to the Italian claims because, while Italy as one of the Axis partners was responsible for bringing on the war against the Allies and for the loss of thousands of Allied lives, Yugoslavia had fought on the Allied side throughout the war and suffered from the attacks of Italy.

As neither the Soviets nor ourselves were prepared to yield, we then proposed that the issue be left to the Peace Conference, but the Soviets would not agree.

This left us in a more serious dilemma than most people realize. We could make a separate peace with Italy, leaving her Trieste, but the Soviet and Yugoslav Governments and possibly others would not accept that treaty.

If we made a separate peace, the Soviet and Yugoslav Governments would undoubtedly demand that Italy make a separate peace with them, ceding Trieste to Yugoslavia. If Italy refused, it is not difficult to foresee the difficulties which would arise.

Even if no one of us presented a treaty to Italy, a disarmed Italy could hold Trieste against the Army of Yugoslavia only so long as our troops held it for her.

In an effort to break this deadlock the French informally suggested that Trieste and adjacent territory be separated from Italy but not ceded to Yugoslavia, and that its security and integrity be internationally guaranteed.

At first no one liked this proposal. But the more it was studied the more it seemed to offer a reasonable basis for agreement. It was recalled that before Italy entered World War I she had proposed that the Trieste area should become an autonomous state.

Our delegation insisted that the area should be protected by the United Nations and not by joint agreement between Italy and Yugoslavia as the Soviets proposed, and not by the four principal Allied powers as suggested by the French. Our proposals were accepted.

The proposal as finally agreed upon leaves Gorizia and Montefalcone with Italy in the north and includes within the free territory of Trieste the rest of the area west of the agreed ethnic line.

It is true that the Free Territory of Trieste is predominantly Italian in the city and predominantly Slav outside of the city. But neither the Italians nor the Slavs in this territory are placed under alien rule. They are given home rule. The people will elect their own Assembly and the Assembly will elect the officials to administer the laws. They will be subject to supervision only by the United Nations Security Council and by an impartial governor appointed by the Security Council.

The prosperity and welfare of Trieste are linked not only with Italy but with Yugoslavia and the countries of central Europe. It is the natural outlet of central Europe to the Mediterranean. The only railroads entering Trieste come through Yugoslavia and are controlled by Yugoslavia. Representatives of that Government asserted that if Trieste were given to Italy they would divert traffic to Fiume or some other port in Yugoslavia.

Because of the bad feeling between the two peoples in that area, the control by the United Nations may prove to be the best means of preventing armed conflict and relieving tension.

If the area were joined either with Italy or Yugoslavia, its political and economic relations with the other would suffer. Its industries might be unable to attract the necessary capital, and labor might have difficulty finding employment.

If friendly relations are maintained between the Free Territory of Trieste and her neighbors, this little territory may enjoy greater prosperity and be a source of greater prosperity to its neighbors than would be the case if it were joined either with Italy or Yugoslavia.

I am convinced that the agreed solution to the problem of Trieste is fair and workable if the peoples most concerned work together to make it so. Unless they work together, there can be no solution.

No final decision was reached on the disposition of the Italian colonies.

It will be recalled that originally the Soviets had requested the trusteeship of Tripolitania. They stated they wanted a base in the Mediterranean for their merchant ships. The French favored Italy as trustee for all the colonies, and at the April session the Soviets expressed their willingness to accept the French proposal. Except for certain reservations in respect of Cyrenaica, the British were willing to accept our proposal to have all the colonies placed under the trusteeship of the United Nations.

In view of the difficulty the Foreign Ministers were having in reaching agreement and the danger of the colonial question becoming a pawn in the settlement of other issues, I suggested that we defer a final decision.

It was finally agreed that the ultimate disposition of the colonies should be made by the four principal Allied powers in light of the wishes and welfare of the inhabitants and world peace and security, taking into account the views of other interested governments.

If the four principal Allied powers do not agree upon the disposition to be made of the colonies within a year after the coming into force of the treaty, they have bound themselves to make such disposition of them as may be recommended by the General Assembly of the United Nations.

The four powers have further agreed to send commissions to the colonies to ascertain the wishes of the local population.

Pending the final disposition of the colonies, they will remain under the existing British military administration.

The thing I like about the agreement on the colonies is that the ultimate decision does not require unanimity. Failing agreement among the four powers, the decision rests with the United Nations.

The Soviets finally withdrew their objection to the cession of the Dodecanese to Greece and to the permanent demilitarization of the Islands.

It was, however, extremely difficult for us to reach agreement on reparations. The Soviets insisted that they were entitled to at least $100,000,000 reparations for the devastation of their territory by the Italian armies.

Moreover, under the armistice agreements with Hungary, Rumania, and Finland reparations payments of $300,000,000 from each had been imposed. The Soviets found it difficult to reconcile themselves to a more lenient reparations policy in the case of Italy.

We on the other hand were more deeply conscious of the help that Italy gave us in the last months of the war and opposed putting on her a reparations burden which would delay her economic recovery.

We had previously agreed that reparations could be taken in war plants not needed for Italian peace-time economy and could be paid out of Italian assets in Hungary, Rumania, and Bulgaria. But the Soviets insisted that part of the reparations should come from current or future production of Italian factories and shipyards.

We reluctantly agreed that the Soviets could receive reparations up to $100,000,000. But we required them to agree that, in so far as reparations were taken from Italian production, the deliveries must be arranged so as to avoid interference with economic reconstruction.

We further required the Soviets to agree that such deliveries should not commence for two years. In order to avoid our having to finance Italy's purchase of raw materials to furnish manufactured products to the Soviets, we also required agreement that the imported materials needed by Italy to make these deliveries should be supplied by the Soviets.

There remain some questions in the Italian treaty and other treaties on which we were unable to reach final agreement. As the Soviet Delegation took the position that they would not agree to the calling of the Peace Conference until the four governments had harmonized their views on fundamental questions, we assume that the Soviets do not regard these issues as fundamental and will accept the decisions of the Peace Conference.

I admit that prior to our meeting in April I had little hope we would ever reach agreement. After our April meeting I had less hope. Now the prospect for peace treaties with five countries is bright. Ninety days after ratification of those treaties occupation armies must be withdrawn except where they protect a line of communications. Then the people of the occupied states can live and breathe as free people. We are on the road back to peace.

I have no desire to conceal from the American people the great struggle and tremendous difficulties the four governments had in harmonizing their views to the extent they did on these treaties. In the long run we shall have a much better chance to work out our problems if we and our Allies recognize the basic differences in our ideas, standards, and methods instead of trying to make ourselves believe that they do not exist or that they are less important than they really are.

While the Council made real progress toward peace with Italy and the ex-satellite states, it made no progress at all on the German and Austrian questions. Perhaps the time taken in discussion was not wholly lost, because our experience suggests that understandings, particularly with our Soviet friends, cannot be reached until we have gone through rounds of verbal combat, in which old complaints are repeated, past positions reaffirmed, differences accentuated, and crises provoked.

I am ready to believe it is difficult for them to understand us, just as it is difficult for us to understand them. But I sometimes think our Soviet friends fear we would think them weak and soft if they agreed without a struggle on anything we wanted, even though they wanted it too. Constant struggle, however, is not always helpful in a world longing for peace.

The Soviets started the German discussion with a prepared statement on the draft treaty we had proposed to guarantee the continued demilitarization and disarmament of Germany for at least a quarter of a century. The Soviet statement reveals how hard-pressed the Soviets were to find real objection to a treaty which gives them the assurance that Germany should never again become a threat to their security or to the security of Europe.

I do not believe that the Soviets realize the doubts and suspicions which they have raised in the minds of those in other countries who want to be their friends by the aloofness, coolness, and hostility with which they have received America's offer to guarantee jointly the continued disarmament of Germany.

Had America been a party to such a guaranty after World War I, World War II would never have occurred, and the Soviet Union would never have been attacked and devastated.

Is German militarism going to be used as a pawn in a struggle between the East and the West, and is German militarism again to be given the chance to divide and conquer?

To that question there must be an unequivocal answer, for equivocation will increase unbearably the tensions and strains which men of good-will everywhere are striving to relieve.

The Soviets stated that our proposed treaty was inadequate; that it did not assure the de-Nazification and democratization of Germany; that it did not assure them reparations. But these are political matters which are already dealt with in the Potsdam Agreement.

Our military agreement of June 5, 1945 provided for the prompt disarmament of armed forces and demilitarization of war plants. By our 25-year treaty we propose that when Germany is once disarmed we shall see that she stays disarmed. We cannot understand Soviet opposition, especially as Generalissimo Stalin on last December 24th agreed with me in principle on this subject.

The Soviet representative stated he had reports that in the British zone the disarming of military forces was not being carried out. The British representative stated he had reports that in the Soviet zone German war plants were being operated.

We asked that the Control Commission investigate the accuracy of both reports. The British and the French agreed. But the Soviet Government would not agree to the investigation unless we limited it to the disarmament of armed forces.

I certainly made clear in our earlier meeting in Paris that the proposed guaranty of German demilitarization was only a part of the German settlement. I proposed then and I proposed again at our recent meeting that deputies be appointed to start work on the whole settlement which the Allies expect the Germans to accept. The British and French accepted the proposal. The Soviets rejected it.

The Soviets suggested that we have a special session of the Council on the German problem. I agreed and insisted on setting a date. But from my experience with the Italian and Balkan settlements I fear that, until the Soviets are willing to have responsible deputies who are in close touch with the Foreign Ministers sit together continuously over a period of time and find out just what is the area of our agreement and our disagreement, the exchange of views between the Ministers on the complicated problems of the German settlement will not be sufficient.

It is no secret that the four-power control of Germany on a zonal basis is not working well from the point of view of any of the four powers. Under the Potsdam Agreement Germany was to be administered as an economic unit and central administrative departments were to be established for this purpose.

But in fact Germany is being administered in four closed compartments with the movement of people, trade, and ideas between the zones more narrowly restricted than between most independent countries.

In consequence none of the zones is self-supporting. Our zone costs our taxpayers $200,000,000 a year. And despite the heavy financial burden being borne by ourselves and other occupying powers, the country is threatened with inflation and economic paralysis.

This condition must not continue. At Paris we proposed that the Control Commission be instructed to establish the central administrative agencies necessary to administer Germany as an economic unit, and to arrange for the exchange of products between the zones and for a balanced program of imports and exports.

The French Government, which had previously opposed the establishment of central administrative agencies, indicated their willingness to accept our proposal when we suggested that the Saar be excluded from the jurisdiction of these agencies. The British agreed.

But the Soviets said that they could not agree to the exclusion of the Saar without further study, and therefore no immediate progress was possible.

I made clear that we were unwilling to share responsibility for the economic paralysis and suffering we felt certain would follow a continuance of present conditions in Germany.

I then announced that as a last resort we were prepared to administer our zone in conjunction with any one or more of the other zones as an economic unit. I indicated that recently we had secured cooperation with the Soviet zone in one matter and with the British in another. I explained that our offer was made not in an effort to divide Germany but to bring it together.

I stated that whatever arrangements were made with one government would be open on equal terms to the governments of the other zones at any time they were prepared to participate.

The British stated that they would consider our proposal and indicated they hoped to agree. Neither the Soviets nor the French expressed any view.

Our military representative in Germany will this week be instructed to cooperate with any one or all of the three governments in essential administrative matters like finance, transportation, communication, trade, and industry. We will either secure economic cooperation between the zones or place the responsibility for the violation of the Potsdam Agreement.

Finally we came to a discussion of the Austrian problem. On June 1, I had circulated a proposed draft treaty recognizing the independence of Austria and providing for the withdrawal of the occupying troops. The British also had submitted a draft for consideration. I asked that the Deputies be directed to prepare the treaty.

The Soviets submitted a counterproposal calling first for further action to insure the de-Nazification of Austria and the removal of a large number of displaced persons from Austria whom they regard as unfriendly to them.

The British and French were willing to join us in submitting to the Deputies the consideration of the treaty and in requesting the Control Council to investigate and report on the progress of de-Nazification and on the problem of the displaced persons. But the Soviets were unwilling to agree to the Deputies' taking up the Austrian treaty until more tangible action was taken on these other two problems.

We recognize the seriousness of these problems and have been grappling with them. The problem of displaced persons is particularly difficult to solve. Where they are willing, we help them to return to their homes. But many refuse to return to their own countries because they fear death or imprisonment for their political views. Our tradition of protecting political refugees is too precious for us to consent to the mass expulsion of these people from our zone. The United Nations has a committee studying the problem, and we shall continue to do our part to try to find a solution, but it cannot be a cruel solution that will reflect discredit upon the American people.

It would be a tragedy to hold up the peace treaty with Austria because she is obliged to afford temporary refuge to these people until homes can be found for them in other countries.

We shall press on in session and out of session to restore conditions of peace to this war-sick world, to bring soldiers back to their homes and to their families, to beat our swords into plowshares. The war has left wounds, but we must work to heal those wounds.

We do not believe in a peace based on a desire for vengeance. We believe in justice, charity, and mercy. If we act with charity and mercy, those we fear as enemies may become our friends. We must trust to the healing processes of peace and pray that God in His mercy will give peace to the world.

APPENDIX 8

Statements by James F. Byrnes, Secretary of State, July 27, 1946

A. *The Prospect for Peace in Europe*

Next Monday at Paris the 21 nations which took an active part in fighting the war against the European Axis will meet to consider treaties of peace with Italy, Finland, Hungary, Bulgaria, and Rumania. The proposed treaties have been drafted by the four principal Allied states. But the Paris conference will carefully review the proposed treaties and after hearing the views of the ex-enemy states will make recommendations to the Council of Foreign Ministers. The Council is obligated to take these recommendations into account and not to reject any of them arbitrarily in drawing up at the close of the conference the final texts of the treaties.

I know that there are many people who believe that it would have been much better if the four principal Allied states did not go to the Conference with agreed texts. But peace treaties that fix boundaries and dispose of colonies and territories cannot be made effective unless they do command the assent of the principal Allied states. If there is no understanding between the principal Allies before the Peace Conference, such understandings must be worked out during the Conference.

Twenty-seven years ago at the Versailles conference the large and the small states came together without any preliminary understanding between the large states. But the principal issues had to be fought out and decided by the Council of the Big Four, and in the end I doubt whether the small states were given as much opportunity to express their views on the concrete peace proposals as will be given the small states at the forthcoming Paris conference. Unfortunately in a world where national states jealously guard their sovereignty, there is no ideal peacemaking procedure.

This is my seventh trip to Europe since I became Secretary of State a year ago. The purpose of each of my journeys has been to speed the return of peace.

From more than one journey I returned with a heavy heart. But after months of persistent effort I am convinced that we are on the road back to peace.

No one is more eager than I to move more speedily along that road.

It is important to begin to withdraw occupation troops wherever the security of the world permits it.   It is important to settle explosive disputes over boundaries and territory.   It is important to fix the reparations bill so that the defeated enemy can begin to pay it off and can see an end to the road.   It is important to get on with the business of providing more food and houses and clothing.

Not until these things are accomplished will the people themselves begin to remember how precious peace really is and to make felt their universal determination not to commit atomic suicide.   It seems to me that the hope of avoiding some new and terrible war greatly depends upon how quickly we can remove the dangerous sources of friction left in the wake of the last war.

For example, as long as the rivalry for Trieste between the Yugoslavs and the Italians continues to mount in intensity and bitterness and to undermine the unity among the larger powers, it is hard for everyone to remember the basic truth that they must hang together or they will hang separately.   Only in calmer days, when men are not blinded by anger and suffering, can they see what a child can see— that their interest in peace is one and indivisible.

These things demonstrate how necessary it is to restore the conditions of peace as quickly as we can.   But they do not eliminate the difficulties that slow the process.   Making the peace is a labor of compromise.   The progress thus far is the product of compromise. There is no use to pretend that more compromises will not be necessary if we are to go the rest of the way.   But the compromises we have reached and those I hope we will reach will be compromises intended to reconcile honest conflicts of opinion and not to secure selfish advantage for ourselves or others.

Whenever a great war is decisively won by Allied nations, the making of peace involves an adjustment and reconciliation of the conflicting views of the victorious nations as to what the peace should be.   We cannot refuse to cooperate just because we cannot write the peace exactly as we would like to write it.

This time we must not only help to make the peace, but we must help to make the peace work.   This time we intend to cooperate with the other nations through the United Nations to build and develop peace.

We are determined that the Paris conference shall be the beginning and not the end of our efforts to build the peace.

B. *Departure from Washington for the Paris Peace Conference*

I APPRECIATE DEEPLY your gathering here to bid me farewell.   I know that your coming here is not a personal tribute to me but is a token of your desire to give expression to the will of the American people to work together to make and to maintain peace.

The situation is entirely different from that which existed after World War I. Then we were badly divided. This time there is no division between the Executive and the Congress as to the making of peace. This time there is no division between the great political parties as to the making of peace.

In our efforts to make peace President Truman and I have had as our co-workers Senator Connally and Senator Vandenberg. The maintenance of peace is a primary task of the Security Council of the United Nations, and to that position the President has appointed a distinguished Republican, Senator Austin of Vermont.

We are all working together, not as partisans of any political party, or of any branch of Government; we are working together as Americans. We are of one mind that America must never return to isolation. However difficult may be the paths of international cooperation, we know there can be no security in isolation.

We are deeply conscious that if we as a nation are to exert our influence on the affairs of the world we must be united. The world cannot rely upon the cooperation of a divided America whose foreign policy is guided by temporary political expediency.

After months of preliminary effort I am hopeful that we will be able at the end of the Paris conference which meets on Monday to sign the first peace treaties.

The signing of peace treaties is only a start, but a very necessary start, on the road back to peace. We must always remember that the maintenance of peace is not dependent solely on the language of a treaty or a series of treaties. Peace must come from the hearts of men and from their willingness to share the blessings of peace with all their neighbors.

The effort to make peace live in the hearts of men has only begun. To that effort a united America must dedicate herself for the sake of her own people and for the sake of all mankind.

APPENDIX 9

Remarks of Senator Tom Connally Before the Political and Territorial Commission for Italy, on the Subject of the Free Territory of Trieste, September 16, 1946

THE CITY of Trieste and its contiguous territory present the most troublesome problem before this Conference. Its proper solution and a wise statute for its government and administration go to the very heart of the peace settlements. This Conference is charged with the responsibility of making such a settlement and of adopting such a wise statute.

The Council of Foreign Ministers agreed upon the establishment of the so-called "French Line" which marks the proposed boundary between Italy and Yugoslavia, between Italy and the Free Territory of Trieste and the proposed boundary between the Free Territory of Trieste and Yugoslavia. The Free Territory of Trieste was to be carved out of this territory to the west of the "French Line". The Council of Foreign Ministers further agrees that the integrity and independence of the Free Territory shall be assured by the Security Council of the United Nations and that the permanent statute for the government of the Free Territory shall be submitted to the Security Council for its approval and its report to the General Assembly of the United Nations.

Among other recommendations of the Council of Foreign Ministers, it was suggested that the Governor shall be appointed by the Security Council, and that legislative and executive authority shall be established on democratic lines under universal suffrage, and that citizens shall be protected with respect to human rights and fundamental freedoms.

The United States Delegation has submitted a proposed draft of the statute for the government of the Free Territory of Trieste which we commend to the study and consideration of the Commission. The United States attaches great importance to the relationship of the Free Territory of Trieste with the Security Council of the United Nations. It is proposed that the constitution of the Free Territory shall be submitted to the Security Council for its approval. This constitution must establish and define the structure of the govern-

114

ment and must contain guaranties to the citizens. We also regard as vital that adequate guaranties must be provided for the absolute independence and integrity of the Free Territory—not alone from Italy and Yugoslavia but from other powers. Its international character must be maintained and protected. It must be strong enough to secure the rights and freedoms of its inhabitants. We hold that the Governor of the Free Territory, who is to be appointed by the Security Council, should be regarded as the agent of the Council and should be entrusted with the power and means to meet the responsibilities placed upon the Security Council. The Governor must possess sufficient power to preserve public order and to insure the observance of the statute for the control of the Free Territory.

The Australian Delegation has expressed doubt as to the authority of the Security Council to perform the duties imposed upon it by these proposals. Article 24, chapter V, of the Charter of the United Nations provides that the Security Council has "primary responsibility for the maintenance of international peace and security". This is a broad grant of authority and carries with it the preserving of international peace and security wherever on the earth either may be threatened. This is ample authority for the exercise of the powers conferred.

The United States proposals envisage election of an assembly for the Free Territory by a popular vote, by universal secret ballot without any discrimination. The statute should also provide methods and means for the territory and for a proper definition respecting the nationality of the inhabitants. There are also economic questions which deserve careful treatment. It is proposed that Trieste shall be a free port, but that will be treated in a special statute. The United States also proposes that the interim government shall be regulated by a provisional statute. It must be elected under thoroughly democratic practices and processes.

Mr. Molotov has proposed that the Free Territory of Trieste and Yugoslavia should be embraced within a customs union. It is the view of the American Delegation that the regulation of customs is a matter for long-term development since the United Nations must bear the deficit in the expenses of the Free Territory. It will no doubt have an interest in the customs arrangements with a possible view of obtaining a source of revenue instead of imposing heavy local property taxes. It is our view that this matter should be worked out at a later date by the Free Territory and the United Nations.

Mr. Molotov expresses a view that under the draft of the United States it might be possible for a foreign government to establish a military base at Trieste. Our proposal is that the Free Territory shall be neutral and demilitarized. It is provided, "No military, naval or air forces, installations or equipment shall be maintained, built, or manufactured in the Free Territory." "No military, naval or air forces of any state shall enter the territory, territorial waters or air space of the Free Territory." These provisions will become effective upon the date on which the permanent statute becomes effective and the free state is created. Under these provisions no armed forces except those of the Security Council, if its authority should be invoked by an incident requiring intervention, would be permitted in the territory. There could be no military or naval bases established.

The proposed text of the treaty articles advanced by the United States may be found in document CP (IT/P) 16. The territory of Trieste must not remain as a danger spot. It must not become a center of irritation and intrigue which may disturb the peace of the world. It must be absolutely independent. Its integrity and dignity must be secured. We are not here to serve the interests of Yugoslavia or the interests of Italy. Yugoslavia and Italy are both subordinate to the peace of the area and to the peace of the world. The Free Territory must not be a satellite of Yugoslavia or Italy. Yugoslavia and Italy must accept and desire that the settlement may be a success. There must be no mental reservations. There must be no secret evasions of mind. If they fail to so accept it they will fail in their duty to the world. Such a course will not advance their own welfare. The peace of the world is more important than a few miles of territory. The peace of the world is more important than inflated national pride.

Since the Security Council of the United Nations is to be given the responsibility to assure the integrity and independence of the Free Territory, it must be endowed with and exercise through the Governor the authority and means to perform this duty. The Free Territory of Trieste must not be merely a "paper state". It must be a real state with its own identity, with its own character, and with its own independence and dignity.

The United States Delegation has also submitted a memorandum in connection with its draft of a proposed statute to which it invites attention. The United States Delegation deems it vital and of imperative importance that a strong and wise statute shall be adopted. This Conference is in search of peace. We are seeking the highways that lead to peace. Europe must do its part for peace. Two world wars have started in Europe. They have involved the rest of the world. The challenge to peace is here. We must not create another Danzig.

The Free Territory of Trieste must in fact be free—free from Yugoslavia and free from Italy. It must be free from intrigue and conspiracy. Its independence must be secure. Its title to existence must be its own. Its authority and power must arise from its own strength. It must be an entity within itself. Let Trieste be a symbol of peace and security.

APPENDIX 10

Address by William L. Clayton, Assistant Secretary of State, August 3, 1946

HERE WE ARE in Paris where for the second time in one generation a delegation from the United States is meeting with delegations from other countries to try to make peace after a great world war. Altogether there are 21 nations represented here—countries which fought the war together against Axis aggression in Europe.

We have got so used to the radio in the last few years that some of my listeners may have forgotten that it was not possible during the drafting of the Versailles Treaty some 27 years ago to talk from Paris to the United States as I am now doing.

In the speech of Secretary Byrnes at the opening of the Paris Peace Conference, we find words which I want to use as my text this evening.

He said: "We want to plant the seeds of future peace and not the seeds of future wars."

The Department of State, where I work, has the responsibility, in conjunction with the President and the Congress, of fixing the foreign policy of the United States Government. My own responsibility relates to the economic aspects of such policy.

The foreign economic policy of the United States is simple. Here it is:

The United States is committed to the support of all sound measures which will contribute to an increase in the production and consumption of goods throughout the world to the end that people everywhere will have more to eat, more to wear, and better homes in which to live.

We do not contend that higher living standards will of themselves guarantee the peace but we do believe that they will create a climate conducive to the preservation of peace in the world.

In order to achieve our objective of a rising standard of living throughout the world, we are committed to the reduction of barriers to the international movement of goods and to the elimination of discriminatory practices in international trade. Such barriers and discriminations sprang up rapidly following the first World War.

The United States Congress has given the President ample authority to deal with these matters through the extension and enlargement of the Hull Reciprocal Trade Agreements Act.

Not only must barriers be lowered and discriminations eliminated if trade is to revive and flourish, but positive action must also be taken for the reconstruction of devastated areas and for the further development of the world's resources.

The Congress of the United States has also acted promptly and adequately in this field through a substantial increase in the lending power of the Export-Import Bank, by ratification of the Bretton Woods agreements, by a contribution of $2,700,000,000 to UNRRA for relief and rehabilitation purposes and by ratification of the credit to Britain. Add to this the foreign credits extended for the purpose of taking over lend-lease inventories and pipe-lines, and sales made or to be made to foreign countries on credit of surplus property, and we reach a grand total of nearly $20,000,000,000 invested by the United States Government since the ending of the war in its effort to assist in the restoration of economic life abroad.

All of which should be sufficient proof of our deep and substantial interest in the economic aspects of the peace treaties now being written here in Paris.

In the economic field, these peace treaties must provide workable settlements of the issues arising out of the war. They must likewise lay a basis for the resumption of normal economic relations between the former enemy states and the United Nations. But many of these problems give rise to conflicting views and interest.

Take, for example, the question of reparations. It is natural that the countries which suffered from aggression should demand reparations from the aggressor, but we must take into account the aggressor's ability to pay. It would do much more harm than good to exact so much of the former enemy that his economic and social structure would be so seriously weakened as to endanger not only his own stability but that of his neighbors as well. We must not repeat the mistakes of the Versailles Treaty.

The peace treaties must deal with a variety of other complicated economic subjects. The most obvious are the claims arising out of the war. In modern warfare all the numerous and complicated relations existing between warring nations in finance, trade, transport, and other fields of economic activity are severed. These relations must be reestablished. The legal position of business enterprises affected by the disruption of relations must be defined. Methods must be provided for the settlement of disputes regarding property relations, patents, shipping, and many other items.

The United States wishes to see these and other war problems settled fairly and promptly. International business relations cannot be restored if there is to be a long period of uncertainty and if assets are to be tied up in protracted litigation for claims procedures. It took many years after the last war to settle many of these problems. The present treaties should provide for speedy settlements so that the former enemy states may promptly resume normal economic relations with the United Nations.

The draft treaties also include provisions of a temporary character governing trade and other economic relations between the former enemies and the United Nations. These provisions, which would assure non-discriminatory treatment, are designed to bridge the gap until new economic agreements can be concluded between the former enemy states and the United Nations. Unlike the provisions of the 1919 treaties on these subjects, which imposed unilateral obligations on the enemy states, the clauses proposed by the Council of Foreign Ministers are reciprocal. The Allies will be entitled under these proposals to fair treatment of their trade and business enterprises only if they in turn grant similar treatment to the enemy states. Agreement on any other basis could not long endure.

Indeed there are many differences between the 1919 treaties and the drafts which are now being considered at this Peace Conference. We have really learned something from experience. One striking difference is in the length of the treaty provisions. In the first World War treaties the economic clauses contain a vast amount of detail and added together make up a book of substantial size. The drafts prepared by the Council of Foreign Ministers are short in comparison. Principles are laid down within the framework of which details can be worked out with the enemy states on a fair basis.

In attempting to deal with future economic relations, the clauses are brief and directed only toward the problems of the first year or so in the post-war period. Many of the rather lengthy and complicated provisions regarding trade, transport, and other matters found in the 1919 treaties are avoided. After the present treaties are concluded, the enemy states will be eligible to apply for admission into the United Nations and into the various international organizations which the United Nations have already created in the economic fields, such as the International Bank, the Monetary Fund, Food and Agriculture Organization, and numerous others.

There are certain economic questions on which the Council of Foreign Ministers did not reach agreement or which the Council felt could be settled only after study and recommendations by the Peace

Conference. These questions include certain aspects of the reparation problem, the status of property relations. Some involve issues of principle. Others involve problems primarily of a technical character. The appropriate commissions of the Conference will doubtless discuss these matters fully and will make recommendations which will facilitate the task of the Council of Foreign Ministers in drawing up the final treaty texts.

The economic provisions of the Versailles peace treaties were full of faults; the economic policies of the nations of the world, ours included, following the first World War were tragically wrong; we broke just about all the rules. No one can say with certainty just how much all of this contributed to the second World War. We do know that it was a powerful factor in the creation of conditions making for war.

In drafting the present treaties we have constantly striven to avoid the mistakes of the past, in the hope that wise economic provisions might help plant the seeds of future peace and not the seeds of future wars.

APPENDIX 11

Remarks of Senator Arthur H. Vandenberg Before the Paris Conference's Economic Commission for the Balkans and Finland, September 30, 1946

THE DELEGATION of the United States has no direct commercial interest in the Danube problem, but we have an emphatic interest in international peace and security and in avoiding international trade barriers which invite discrimination and friction. These factors here involved have a special temporary interest in the Danube because it is an important—and now stagnant—artery of commerce in the American zones of occupation in Germany and Austria. Therefore we feel entitled to urge these general principles for a free international Danube as contained in the U.S. and U.K. proposal.

As regards our temporary interest, it is well known that we want Germany administered as an economic unit pursuant to the unmistakable Potsdam mandate for the benefit of the total German economy. It is historically clear that Danubian commerce cannot prosper if it is at the mercy of various uncoordinated, restrictive, and discriminatory administrations which respond to the local judgments of the eight national jurisdictions through which the Danube flows. Some of the troublesome current problems on the Danube are the result of thus dividing the Danube in watertight compartments. So long, therefore, as American occupation continues in Germany and Austria, we are "parties in interest"—although it is a very unselfish interest.

But our basic concern is something else. Here is the longest navigable waterway in Europe west of the Soviet Union. It is important to the commerce of eight riparian states and to the commerce of many other states. It has long involved other significant impacts upon central Europe. As was once said of the Thames, the Danube is "liquid history".

Such a stream is an inevitable factor in the peace of the area it serves; therefore it is a factor in the total and indivisible peace which we are all pledged to sustain.

The Danube River system is of great importance in the exchange of commodities among the nations in the Danube basin and as a means of contact with the outside world. Its significance as an artery of trade is enhanced by the comparative inadequacy of rail and highway

122

facilities in this area. These things are important to all of us, because the restoration of a sound economy is prerequisite to a sound peace. It is impossible to contemplate a prosperous Danube without an over-all assurance of navigation and commerce free from discriminations and arbitrary sectional barriers. It is equally impossible otherwise to contemplate a peaceful Danube, because it is historically a zone of friction.

These are old truths. They have been recognized by the mainte-nance of international administration of the Danube in differing degrees since 1856. The Treaty of Versailles internationalized the Danube, for example, from the head of navigation to the sea and established free navigation throughout the river's length with a con-trol commission including other than riparian states as a recognition of the breadth of interest involved.

It is needless to trace the fluctuating fortunes of the various Danu-bian commissions since 1856. The important point in the American view is that this relative freedom of navigation on the Danube has been accepted in one form or another as essential for 90 years. It is obviously even more essential in this new era when the United Nations are making common cause for peace and progress.

The pending proposal, Mr. President, declares a set of general principles. Navigation shall be free and open on terms of equality to all states. Laws and regulations shall be non-discriminatory. No obstacles to navigation shall be placed in the main channels. No tolls or other charges shall be levied except to defray the costs of develop-ment and maintenance, and the latter shall be administered in such a manner as not to discriminate against any state. Equality is guar-anteed Rumania in any international regime. In addition to these general principles a conference of all interested states shall meet within six months to establish this regime. Any disagreements will be umpired by the International Court of Justice.

Mr. President, so far as these general principles are concerned, I venture to say that they have been inherent in the Danubian regime in one form or another throughout these 90 years. This is no new concept. It has been acknowledged as the essential formula for peace and progress—no matter how illy implemented—for almost a century. It seems to the American Delegation that it would be a great mistake for us to turn our backs upon all this history and experience. Worse, our silence would be an actual retreat—an abandonment of freedoms long established before we fought World War II for great freedoms. It seems to us that the world is entitled to know that its peacemakers are at least "holding their own" and not slipping back into darker ages.

We agree that riparian states have a special interest, but all riparian states except enemy states are represented at this table. The others have a right of consultation under this proposal in developing these plans unless we intend to repudiate history and experience which we do not anticipate. It seems to us we should welcome an opportunity in this Rumanian treaty to pledge Rumania to these general principles, particularly in view of the fact that it was Rumania which upset the fairly satisfactory international regime in 1938 by demanding a rendition to herself to the substantive powers of the then existing Danube Commission.

In a word, Mr. President, it seems to the American Delegation that if we intend that the Danube shall resume the freedoms heretofore established and shall develop in peace and progress we must say so now. It is our only chance. We shall not collide with any Danubian aspirations unless these aspirations collide with these freedoms. In such an unexpected event it is doubly necessary that we should anticipate the protective contract now.

For these reasons the United States Delegation has joined with the proposal of the United Kingdom in its present or in any perfected form.

Regarding the draft peace treaty with Rumania, part VII, article 34, Clauses relating to the Danube, a redraft submitted September 27 by the U.K. and U.S. Delegations of article 34 to supersede the existing U.S. and U.K. drafts reads as follows:

"A. Paragraphs 1 through 6 are exactly the same as in the draft peace treaty with Rumania. There is added one paragraph reading: 'B. A conference consisting of U.S., U.S.S.R., U.K., and France together with the riparian states including Rumania will be convened within a period of six months of the coming into force of the present treaty to establish the new permanent international regime for the Danube'."

APPENDIX 12

The Paris Peace Conference, Report by James F. Byrnes, Secretary of State, October 18, 1946

IT IS NOW 15 months since the decision was reached at Potsdam to set up the Council of Foreign Ministers to start the preparatory work on the peace treaties with Italy, Bulgaria, Rumania, Hungary, and Finland.

Those months have been hard, difficult months.

At the Council of Foreign Ministers and at the Paris Peace Conference your representatives were a united and harmonious delegation acting under the guidance and instructions of the President of the United States. The difficult tasks were immeasurably lightened by the splendid work and cooperation of my associates, Senator Connally, Democratic chairman of the Foreign Relations Committee, and Senator Vandenberg, spokesman for the Republican Party in foreign affairs. In the Conference we have represented no political parties. We have been united in representing the United States.

After every great war the victorious allies have found it difficult to adjust their differences in the making of peace. Even before the fighting stopped, President Roosevelt warned us that

"The nearer we came to vanquishing our enemies the more we inevitably became conscious of differences among the allies."

That was why President Roosevelt was so insistent that the United Nations should be established before the peace settlements were made.

It was inevitable that in the making of concrete peace settlements the Allies should discuss and debate the issues on which they disagree and not those on which they agree. It was also inevitable that such discussions should emphasize our differences.

That is one reason I have continuously pressed to bring about agreements upon the peace settlements as rapidly as possible.

Leaving unsettled issues which should be settled only serves to increase tension among the Allies and increase unrest among the peoples affected.

We cannot think constructively on what will or will not contribute to the building of lasting peace and rising standards of life until we liquidate the war and give the peoples of this world a chance to live again under conditions of peace.

It is difficult to deal with the problems of a convalescing world until we get the patient off the operating table.

These treaties are not written as we would write them if we had a free hand. They are not written as other governments would write them if they had a free hand. But they are as good as we can hope to get by general agreement now or within any reasonable length of time.

Our views on reparations are different from the views of countries whose territories were laid waste by military operations and whose peoples were brought under the yoke of alien armies and alien gestapos.

The reparation payments are heavy—excessively heavy in some cases. But their burdens should not be unbearable if the peoples on which they are laid are freed from the burdens of sustaining occupying armies and are given a chance to rebuild their shattered economic lives.

For Europe with her mingled national economies there are no ideal boundary settlements.

The proposed settlement for the Trieste area was long and warmly debated. The Conference approved the proposal of the Council of Foreign Ministers that this area should become a free territory under the protection of the United Nations. The Conference also by a two-thirds vote made recommendations for an international statute defining the responsibilities of the United Nations in relation to the free territory. Such recommendations are an expression of world opinion and cannot be arbitrarily disregarded.

Those recommendations of the Conference provide that the governor appointed by the Security Council should have sufficient authority to maintain public order and security, to preserve the independence and integrity of the territory, and to protect the basic human rights and fundamental freedoms of all the inhabitants.

The minority proposal which was supported by the Soviet Union, Yugoslavia, and other Slav countries would have made a figurehead of the United Nations governor and would have given Yugoslavia virtual control of the customs, currency, and foreign affairs of the territory. Certainly we could not agree to that. It would make the territory a protectorate of Yugoslavia and would leave the United Nations powerless to prevent it becoming a battleground between warring groups. There must be no seizure of power in Trieste after this war as there was in Fiume after the last war.

The Yugoslav Delegation advised the Conference it would not sign the treaty recommended. My hope however is that after consideration Yugoslavia will realize that just as other states have made concessions she must make concessions in order to bring about the peace.

Although the Council of Foreign Ministers were unable to agree to any change in the Austrian-Italian frontier, the representatives of Austria and Italy at Paris were encouraged by the American Delegation to reach an agreement which should help to make the South Tyrol a bond rather than a barrier between the two peoples.

It is my earnest hope that Czechoslovakia and Hungary and Rumania and Hungary may find by common agreement somewhat similar solutions to their complicated nationality problems on the basis of working together as friends and as neighbors. We in America know that people of many different races and stocks can live together in peace in the United States. They should be able to live together in peace in Europe.

At Potsdam in the summer of 1945 President Truman stressed the importance of providing for free navigation of the great international rivers in Europe on terms of equality for the commerce of all states.

President Truman was not seeking any special advantage for the United States. He was seeking to promote peace. He was seeking to ensure that these great waterways should be used to unite and not divide the peoples of Europe.

The Delegations representing the Soviet Republic and the Slav countries have vigorously opposed the proposal.

The Paris Conference recommended by a two-thirds vote that the treaties should ensure freedom of commerce on the Danube on terms of equality to all states.

I hope that when the Foreign Ministers meet we can agree upon the adoption of this recommendation.

In recent weeks much has been said about acrimonious debates and the divisions in the Paris Conference. Back of these debates and divisions were real and deep differences in interest, in ideas, in experience, and even in prejudices.

Those differences cannot be dispelled or reconciled by a mere gloss of polite words. And in a democratic world those differences cannot and should not be kept from the peoples concerned.

In a democratic world, statesmen must share with the people their trials as well as their triumphs.

It is better that the world should witness and learn to appraise clashes of ideas rather than clashes of arms.

If this peace is to be lasting, it must be a people's peace; and the peoples of this world who long for peace will not be able to make their influence felt if they do not know the conflict in ideas and in interest that give rise to war, and if they do not know how the statesmen and the peoples of other countries view those conflicts.

But it is our hope that in international democracy, as in national democracy, experience will prove that appeals to reason and good faith which unite people count for more in the long run than appeals to prejudice and passion which divide people.

In a world where no sovereign state can be compelled to sign or ratify a peace treaty, there is no perfect peacemaking machinery. Where boundaries, colonies, and reparations are involved, a peace treaty cannot be made effective unless it is satisfactory to the principal powers.

Under these circumstances the Paris Conference provided as adequate an opportunity for the smaller states and the ex-enemy states to express their views on the proposed treaties as it was practical to provide.

The thing which disturbs me is not the lettered provisions of the treaties under discussion but the continued if not increasing tension between us and the Soviet Union.

The day I took office as Secretary of State I stated that "the supreme task of statesmanship the world over is to help the people of this war-ravaged earth to understand that they can have peace and freedom only if they tolerate and respect the rights of others to opinions, feelings and ways of life which they do not and cannot share."

It is as true now as it was then that the development of sympathetic understanding between the Soviet Union and the United States is the paramount task of statesmanship.

Such understanding is necessary to make the United Nations a true community of nations.

From the Potsdam Conference, which took place at the beginning of his administration, President Truman and I have worked and we shall continue to work to bring about an understanding with the Soviet Government.

Two states can quickly reach an understanding if one is willing to yield to all demands. The United States is unwilling to do that. It is equally unwilling to ask it of another state.

Every understanding requires the reconciliation of differences and not a yielding by one state to the arbitrary will of the other.

Until we are able to work out definite and agreed standards of conduct such as those which govern decisions within the competence of the International Court of Justice, and such as those which we hope may be agreed upon for the control of atomic energy, international problems between sovereign states must be worked out by agreement between sovereign states.

But if states are to reach such agreements they must act in good faith and in the spirit of conciliation. They must not launch false and misleading propaganda against one another.

They must not arbitrarily exercise their power of veto, preventing a return to conditions of peace and delaying economic reconstruction. No state should assume that it has a monopoly of virtue or of wisdom. No state should ignore or veto the aggregate sentiments of mankind.

States must not unilaterally by threats, by pressures, or by force disturb the established rights of other nations. Nor can they arbitrarily resist or refuse to consider changes in the relationships between states and peoples which justice, fair play, and the enlightened sentiments of mankind demand.

We must cooperate to build a world order, not to sanctify the *status quo*, but to preserve peace and freedom based upon justice.

And we must be willing to cooperate with one another—veto or no veto—to defend, with force if necessary, the principles and purposes of the Charter of the United Nations.

Those are the policies we have pursued. In following those policies we have been criticized at times for being too "soft" and at times for being too "tough". I dislike both words. Neither accurately describes our earnest efforts to be patient but firm.

We have been criticized for being too eager to find new approaches after successive rebukes in our efforts to effectuate our policies. And we have likewise been criticized for not seeking new approaches. We will not permit the criticism to disturb us nor to influence our action.

We will continue to seek friendship with the Soviet Union and all other states on the basis of justice and the right of others, as well as ourselves, to opinions and ways of life which we do not and cannot share.

But we must retain our perspective.

We must guard against the belief that deep-rooted suspicions can be dispelled and far-reaching differences can be reconciled by any single act of faith.

The temple of peace must be built solidly, stone upon stone. If the stones are loosely laid, they may topple down upon us.

We must equally guard against the belief that delays or set-backs in achieving our objective make armed conflict inevitable. It is entirely possible that the failure or inability of the Soviet leaders to rid themselves of that belief lies at the very root of our difficulties. We will never be able to rid the world of that belief if we ourselves become victims to it.

For centuries devout men and women thought it was necessary to fight with one another to preserve their different religious beliefs. But through long and bitter experience they learned that the only way to protect their own religious beliefs is to respect and recognize the rights of others to their religious beliefs.

War is inevitable only if states fail to tolerate and respect the rights of other states to ways of life they cannot and do not share. That is a truth we must all recognize.

Because in the immediate aftermath of war our efforts to induce nations to think in terms of peace and tolerance seem to meet with rebuff, we must not lose faith. What may be unrealizable now may be realizable when the wounds of war have had a chance to heal.

We must not lose faith nor cease to struggle to realize our faith, because the temple of peace cannot be completely built in a month or a year.

But if the temple of peace is to be built the idea of the inevitability of conflict must not be allowed to dominate the minds of men and tear asunder a world which God made one.

It is that idea of the inevitability of conflict that is throttling the economic recovery of Europe. It is that idea that is causing artificial tensions between states and within states.

The United States stands for freedom for all nations and for friendship among all nations. We shall continue to reject the idea of exclusive alliances. We shall refuse to gang up against any state.

We stand with all peace-loving, law-abiding states in defense of the principles of the Charter of the United Nations.

Any nation that abides by those principles can count upon the friendship and cooperation of the United States, irrespective of national differences or possible conflict of interests.

No country desires unity among the principal powers more than we or has done more to achieve it. But it must be unity founded on the Charter and not unity purchased at its expense.

We deplore the tendency upon the part of the Soviet Union to regard states which are friendly to us as unfriendly to the Soviet Union and to consider as unfriendly our efforts to maintain traditionally friendly relations with states bordering on the Soviet Union.

We deplore the talk of the encirclement of the Soviet Union. We have it from no less authority than Generalissimo Stalin himself that the Soviet Union is in no danger of encirclement.

During the war the Baltic states were taken over by the U.S.S.R. The Polish frontier and the Finnish frontier have been substantially modified in Russia's favor. Königsberg, Bessarabia, Bukovina, and Ruthenia are to be given to her. In the Pacific, the Kuriles, Port Arthur, and Sakhalin have been assigned to her. Certainly the Soviet Union is not a dispossessed nation.

We know the suffering and devastation which Nazi aggression brought to the Soviet Union. The American people came to the support of the Soviet Union even before the United States was attacked and entered the war. Our people were allies of the Soviet people during the war. And the American people in time of peace desire to live on terms of friendship, mutual helpfulness, and equality with the Soviet people.

Before the Paris Peace Conference the United States spared no effort to reconcile its views on the proposed treaties with the views of the Soviet Union. Indeed it was the Soviet Union which insisted that our views be reconciled on all questions which the Soviet Union regarded as fundamental before they would consent to the holding of the Conference.

If, therefore, in the Conference we differed on some questions, they were not questions that were fundamental from the Soviet viewpoint.

While there were many issues which attracted little public attention on which the Soviet Union and the United States voted together, it was regrettable that on many issues which did command public attention the Soviet Union and the newly established governments in central and southeastern Europe voted consistently together against all the other states.

Whatever considerations caused this close alignment of the Soviet Union and her Slav neighbors on these issues, other states were not constrained to vote as they did by any caucus or bloc action.

It requires a very imaginative geographic sense to put China or Ethiopia into a Western bloc. And it was quite evident to discerning observers at Paris that not only China and Ethiopia, but Norway and France were particularly solicitous to avoid not only the fact, but the suspicion, of alliance with any Western bloc.

If the voting cleavage at Paris was significant, its significance lies in the fact that the cleavage is not between the United States and the Soviet Union, or between a Western bloc and the Soviet Union. The cleavage is based upon conviction and not upon strategy or hidden design.

I should be less than frank if I did not confess my bewilderment at the motives which the Soviet Delegation attributed to the United

States at Paris. Not once, but many times, they charged that the United States had enriched itself during the war, and, under the guise of freedom for commerce and equality of opportunity for the trade of all nations, was now seeking to enslave Europe economically.

Coming from any state these charges would be regrettable to us. They are particularly regrettable when they are made by the Soviet Government to whom we advanced more than 10 billion dollars of lend-lease during the war and with whom we want to be friendly in time of peace.

The United States has never claimed the right to dictate to other countries how they should manage their own trade and commerce. We have simply urged in the interest of all peoples that no country should make trade discriminations in its relations with other countries.

On that principle the United States stands. It does not question the right of any country to debate the economic advantages or disadvantages of that principle. It does object to any government charging that the United States enriched itself during the war and desires to make "hand-outs" to European governments in order to enslave their peoples.

Long before we entered the war President Roosevelt took the dollar sign out of the war. He established lend-lease as the arsenal of democracy and opened that arsenal to all who fought for freedom. Europe did not pay and was not asked to pay to build or to replenish that arsenal. That was done with American labor and American resources.

The lend-lease settlements inaugurated by President Roosevelt have been faithfully and meticulously carried out by President Truman.

We want to assist in European reconstruction because we believe that European prosperity will contribute to world prosperity and world peace. That is not dollar democracy. That is not imperialism. That is justice and fair play.

We in America have learned that prosperity like freedom must be shared, not on the basis of "hand-outs," but on the basis of the fair and honest exchange of the products of the labor of free men and free women.

America stands for social and economic democracy at home and abroad. The principles embodied in the social and economic reforms of recent years are now a part of the American heritage.

It would be strange indeed if in this imperfect world our social and economic democracy were perfect, but it might help our Soviet friends to understand us better if they realized that today our social and economic democracy is further away from the devil-take-the-hindmost philosophy of by-gone days than Soviet Russia is from Tsarist Russia. Whatever political differences there may be among us, we are firmly and irrevocably committed to the principle that it is our right and the right of every people to organize their economic and political destiny through the freest possible expression of their collective will. We oppose privilege at home and abroad. We defend freedom everywhere. And in our view human freedom and human progress are inseparable.

The American people extend the hand of friendship to the people of the Soviet Union and to all other people in this war-weary world. May God grant to all of us the wisdom to seek the paths of peace.

APPENDIX 13

Excerpts From a Radio Interview With Senator Arthur H. Vandenberg, October 19, 1946

. . . . . .

THE 21 ALLIES have now made their recommendations respecting treaties with Italy, Rumania, Bulgaria, Hungary, and Finland. These recommendations go to the Council of Foreign Ministers of the four big powers for the final decisions. Here there will be new difficulties. But solutions are on their way. . . . Of course none of us is wholly satisfied with the treaty recommendations. But here at least is the world's verdict on the controversies in these treaties—and that is progress. . . .

We agreed (at the Paris Conference) upon the principles of a sound statute for Trieste—the cockpit of Europe—a statute which sustains our American view that there can be no peace unless Trieste is free and independent and democratic in fact as well as name.

Again: we agreed upon the principles for a free Danube river, vital to peace and progress in eight nations—principles which support our contention that this major artery of trade in central Europe shall not operate under selfish discriminations which breed inevitable frictions.

Again: we agreed upon reparations and restitutions—a program which at least partially reflects *our* anxiety that these ex-enemy states shall pay as much as possible toward rehabilitation of the war damage they have done, but that their burdens shall not become unlivable and therefore uncollectable.

We revised our own demands for 100 percent compensation for American property destroyed in ex-enemy states and joined the Soviets in supporting partial compensation because there can only be partial, and not full, reparations or restitution.

We agreed upon numerous new boundaries.

One happy omen was that Italy and Austria mutually agreed upon compromises in the South Tyrol.

Then there were countless details respecting all phases of human relations—all parts of one big jigsaw puzzle. You must remember that a peace treaty is not a simple contract covering a few pages. It is literally a book. Let me give you one typical example. The final meeting of our Balkan Economic Committee of which I was a member consumed 28½ uninterrupted hours and involved 88 roll calls. And it is worth remembering that we had friendly unity 75 percent of the time. I do not minimize the desperate importance of the other 25 percent. A chain is no stronger than its weakest link. But neither am I willing to minimize the fact that our minds did meet 75 percent of the time.

We must not forget that hammering out a multiple peace has always been "confusing" and has always taken time and patience. More than a century ago, the Congress of Vienna sat upon a similar but simpler job for more than one full year. After all, it took five years to tear the world apart. It is not surprising if it takes that long to put it together again. The Paris Conference is part of this process. I have no illusions about the perilous difficulties we confront. But I want to make equally plain that I am not surrendering to pessimism. Many of the Paris speeches were in good temper, despite deep disagreements. I quote one of Mr. Molotov's comments. Deploring divisions among us, he said, "We need not doubt that we shall meet the desires of all peace-loving peoples." I join that prayer. In the same connection I also quote the final, significant sentence in a recent metropolitan editorial: "If Russia is willing to honor in victory what she signed when in need of help, the division which Mr. Molotov deplores will disappear over night." We must be sure we, too, are as faithful to every commitment we have made. . . . The German and Austrian treaties will be the key to post-war Europe. We have been pressing for a start upon these treaties for many months. I regret to say there is still no agreement with the Soviets regarding Austria. But there is agreement that the German discussions shall start in November. That, again, is at least some progress. . . . I hear much more war-talk over here than I did in Paris. I'm afraid we have too many American groups which over-zealously seek to make their own peace ideas impressive by using war as the frightening alternative. I wish we could quit talking about "war". In my opinion, if it happens it will come from some tragically unfortunate incident which may well be the result of somebody's miscalculation as to how far we will tolerate some policy which either threatens our own security or world peace or which violates our conception of human rights and funda- mental freedoms. That is why, in my view, it is so vitally necessary that we should be wholly frank with Russia—say what we mean and mean what we say. Candor must not be mistaken for ill will. And that, too, is why we must have, so far as self-serving politicians will permit, a united American foreign policy, supported generally by Republicans and Democrats alike, so there will be no delusion abroad that we are vulnerable because we are at the mercy of internal divisions. In other words, we must not be responsible for any "miscalculations". That way, I dare to hope, lies peace—particularly with the United Nations to cushion the impact even of "miscalculations." This much is certain. America's bipartisan foreign policy today is not a policy of war. It is a policy of peace. In my opinion, it will succeed—unless it is scuttled here at home. . . .

I like a phrase in the resolutions just adopted by the national convention of the American Legion: "American foreign policy should be neither hostile nor subservient to any other Power on earth." And if you'll allow me just one second of personal latitude . . . I also like the following sentence from the American Legion's Resolutions:

"We strongly endorse and support the positive foreign policy of the Government of the United States as expressed by Secretary of State Byrnes, Senator Vandenberg and Senator Connally."

. . . Imperfect as the Security Council and the General Assembly of the United Nations may be . . . they are the justified hope of the world. They provide a medium of contact where we can all come to know each other better; where, perhaps, we can learn to "live and let live"; and where, if the unhappy climax requires, we can mobilize the vast majority of mankind against the next aggressor who threatens peace and security and human rights and fundamental freedoms. Who shall say that the agencies of the United Nations cannot bridge the gap between the East and West? The United Nations will continue to have plenty of growing pains. But, I repeat, their effective evolution is the hope of the world—and the darker gathering clouds may be, the greater the need for this sunshine to break through.

APPENDIX 14

The Third Session of the Council of Foreign Ministers in New York, November 4–December 12, 1946, Report by Charles E. Bohlen, Special Assistant to the Secretary of State

I· Completion of Texts of Treaties of Peace With Italy, Rumania, Bulgaria, Hungary, and Finland

THE THIRD SESSION of the Council of Foreign Ministers which was held in New York City at the Waldorf-Astoria Hotel from November 4 to December 12, 1946, finally completed the texts of the treaties of peace with Italy, Rumania, Bulgaria, Hungary, and Finland. These texts have now been published and will be presented on February 10, 1947, for signature by the representatives of the states which participated in the Paris Peace Conference and which were at war with the enemy states in question. The United States was not at war with Finland and consequently will not be a party to the peace treaty with Finland. They will enter into force immediately upon ratification by the Allied states signatories to the respective armistices and by France in the case of Italy.

Although it had been hoped that time would permit the Council of Foreign Ministers to draw up final texts of these treaties in Paris following the close of the Paris Peace Conference, this task proved to be impossible in view of the forthcoming meeting of the General Assembly of the United Nations in New York, which certain of the Foreign Ministers desired to attend in person. Secretary of State Byrnes therefore invited the Council of Foreign Ministers to meet in New York concurrently with the General Assembly in order to avoid any further delay in the completion of these five peace treaties. The purpose of this session of the Council of Foreign Ministers, which was the third devoted to the drafting of these peace treaties, was to consider the recommendations of the Paris Peace Conference and to endeavor to agree upon the final texts.

Secretary Byrnes had since the April–May meeting of the Council of Foreign Ministers urged the calling of the Paris Peace Conference, which met from July 29 until October 15, believing that all members of the United Nations who had participated actively in military operations against the European members of the Axis were entitled to be given a full opportunity to make known their views and to have those views taken into consideration. Furthermore, the members of the Council of Foreign Ministers had solemnly agreed to "give the fullest consideration" to and "not reject arbitrarily" the recommendations from this Conference. Secretary Byrnes had also pointed out on a number of occasions that the recommendations of this Conference should be of great assistance to the Council of Foreign Ministers in finding solutions to the issues on which they had been unable to agree.

The Paris Peace Conference, through long discussion both in the commissions and in plenary sessions, had given the fullest possible consideration to every aspect of the peace treaties and had adopted 59 recommendations by two-thirds majority and 48 recommendations by a simple majority. For the most part, these recommendations related to questions which the Council of Foreign Ministers, despite protracted negotiation and discussion, had left in disagreement or had not considered. Thus the third session of the Council of Foreign Ministers in considering those issues which had previously divided the Council and Conference had the advantage of formal recommendations on these and other issues by the 21 nations at the Paris Conference. These recommendations and especially those backed by two thirds of the members of the Conference were a new factor in the work of the Council of Foreign Ministers and played a large if not determinant part in settling the still unsolved issues in these treaties. In effect the final texts of these treaties reveal that on the majority of issues final agreement was based upon the recommendations returned to the Council of Foreign Ministers by the Paris Conference.

This agreement was particularly evident in regard to the draft statute of the Free Territory of Trieste. Although the Council of Foreign Ministers last July had reached an agreement on the internationalization under the United Nations of this territory and on its proposed boundaries, no agreement had been reached by the special Commission on Trieste appointed by the Council of Foreign Ministers on the principles which were to govern the temporary regime and on the permanent statute for the area. Secretary Byrnes had made it clear that the United States, having agreed—contrary to its original position—to the internationalization of this area, was determined that the proposed Free Territory should be genuinely international in character and not a hotbed of friction and dispute between Italy and Yugoslavia. In view of the tension existing in the area and the rivalry between these two countries, the United States believed it to be essential that the representatives of the Security

Council and the United Nations who were to assume responsibility for the integrity and security of this area must have adequate powers to discharge these responsibilities. As a neutral figure—representative of the United Nations as a whole—the proposed Governor for the Free Territory of Trieste would have no interest except to safeguard the security of the area and to promote the well-being and preserve the rights and freedoms of the inhabitants. The representatives of Great Britain and France had held similar views. The Soviet representative, however, had supported the claims of Yugoslavia to a special and privileged position in this territory and had opposed the granting to the Governor and to the United Nations what the United States regarded as absolutely essential powers for the maintenance of the international character and stability of the area. By a two-thirds vote the Paris Conference recommended the adoption of a French compromise proposal setting forth the principles for the organization of the Free Territory of Trieste, which were in basic accord with the views of the British and American Governments.

At the New York session of the Council of Foreign Ministers the principles for the permanent statute and provisional regime of the Free Territory of Trieste as recommended by the Conference were incorporated in a final draft after protracted negotiation. The statute as finally agreed upon has been incorporated as an annex to the peace treaty for Italy. If backed by an honest intention on the part of the states directly concerned to implement this statute as written, it provides the framework for the creation and maintenance of a genuine international regime for this troublesome and disputed area.

After agreement on the statute for the Free Territory of Trieste had been reached, the only other questions of importance still in dispute related to reparations, other economic clauses, and the question of freedom of navigation on the Danube River.

The reparation problem proved to be one of the most difficult. Marked difference in attitude existed between countries which had been devastated by one or another of these ex-enemy states and which therefore felt entitled to the maximum amounts possible, and between countries like the United States which felt that the most important thing was to build for a future in which the ex-enemy states would have some prospect of economic recovery. In the cases of Rumania, Hungary, and Finland, the reparation terms as set forth in their armistices provided for $300,000,000 of commodities at 1938 prices. Although the United States argued at great length that these three countries were not identical in the degree of their aggression nor equal in their capacity to pay, this Government was unable to obtain any change in the established arrangements which had already been implemented by bilateral agreements. In the case of Bulgaria, where the reparation terms were not fixed in the armistice, the situation was reversed, the Soviet Union arguing for an extremely low reparation obligation. Actually, the figure of $70,000,000 which was agreed on is not far out of line when compared with the obligation of Rumania, but it does throw into sharp contrast the burden of reparations placed on Hungary and Finland.

The problem of reparation is much simpler in the case of those four countries which were all net exporters than in the case of Italy. In order to find a practical means for payment by Italy, the formula previously agreed upon for Italian reparation to the Union of Soviet Socialist Republics—namely, that the reparation-receiving country must supply the required raw material—was utilized in connection with the other recipients. There were two particularly difficult problems: that of the relative treatment of Greece and Yugoslavia and that of whether Albania should be included at all. The first problem was resolved by giving Greece and Yugoslavia each the same total amount of $150,000,000 from Bulgaria and Italy. The second problem was resolved by giving a smaller payment of $5,000,000 to Albania.

It is also important to note that the commercial-policy provisions which this Government has urged from the very start are now incorporated in the treaties. These provisions establish, for a period of 18 months, an obligation on the part of the ex-enemy state not to discriminate among nations in matters pertaining to commerce and industry. This requirement is limited to 18 months in order to permit the concluding of commercial treaties. Furthermore, that period of time should determine whether international trade throughout the world will follow the liberal principles outlined in the American proposals for the expansion of world trade or whether various countries themselves will revert to discriminatory and restrictive-trade regulation. A similar provision with respect to aviation rights, including the first two freedoms of the air, is included in each treaty.

The question of including a clause expressing acceptance of the principle of free navigation on that great European waterway in the peace treaties with the ex-enemy states bordering on the Danube had been the subject of long dispute and acrimonious debate at previous sessions of the Council of Foreign Ministers, particularly at the Paris Peace Conference. In this case again the Conference had voted by a two-thirds majority for the inclusion in the appropriate treaties of some statement of the important principle of free navigation. It is gratifying to report that at the New York meeting the Soviet objections on this score were overcome, and the three Balkan treaties include the following statement of principle: "Navigation on the Danube shall be free and open for the nationals, vessels of commerce, and goods of all States, on a footing of equality in regard to port and navigation charges and conditions for merchant shipping." In order to reduce this general principle to specific operation, the Council of Foreign Ministers has agreed to call a conference within six months in which the United States, Great Britain, the Soviet Union, and France would participate, as well as the countries in the Danubian basin, for the purpose of establishing an international regime with respect to the Danube. The United States has very little direct interest in the Danube as such. The great concern of the United States has been to do all that it could to remove artificial barriers and discriminatory practices from national trade regulations and specifically from this vital waterway in southeastern Europe.

Other economic articles which dealt with such problems as restitution, compensation for damages, ex-enemy property in the United Nations, and the reinstatement of debt obligations posed certain difficulties of one kind or another; however, it is believed that the interests of the United States have been safeguarded so far as possible under the circumstances.

After more than 15 months since the opening session of the Council of Foreign Ministers set up by the Potsdam Conference to draft in the first instance treaties of peace with Italy and the former satellite states, the final texts of these treaties have now been completed. It cannot be said that the treaties themselves are entirely satisfactory, and, as Secretary Byrnes said in discussing the drafts presented to the Peace Conference, they are "not the best which human wit could devise", but they do represent the best which could be reached by unanimous agreement among the members of the Council of Foreign Ministers. When they enter into effect, despite their imperfections, they will be the first real step forward toward the return to normal peacetime conditions for these countries. They will bring to an end armistice regimes giving to the occupying power almost unlimited control over the national life of these countries, and they will, in some cases, mean the complete withdrawal of and, in others, major reduction in the occupying forces which, since the end of the war, have imposed such heavy burdens on their national economies. Finally, the treaties will permit Italy, Rumania, Bulgaria, Hungary, and Finland to reassume their responsibilities as sovereign states in international affairs and will afford them an opportunity to qualify for membership in the organization of the United Nations.

II. *Preliminary Plans for Peace Settlements With Germany and Austria*

In addition to completing final texts of the five peace treaties the Council of Foreign Ministers, as had been agreed in Paris, devoted several meetings of its New York session to the German and Austrian questions. As early as May 1946 Secretary Byrnes had endeavored without success to obtain agreement for the setting up of special deputies to start the preliminary work for the eventual peace settlement with Germany and to prepare a draft settlement with Austria so that without undue delay the Council of Foreign Ministers could take up these two questions vital to the entire future of Europe. The Soviet Government in May and again in July had been unwilling to agree to these proposals and had maintained that further study was required before deputies could be appointed to begin actual work concerning either a future German settlement or an Austrian treaty. At the New York session, however, these objections were overcome, and the following are the main points in the agenda adopted for the next meeting of the Council of Foreign Ministers to be held in Moscow on March 10, 1947:

1. Consideration of the report from the Allied Control Council;
2. Consideration of the form and scope of the provisional political organization of Germany;
3. Preparation of a peace treaty with Germany, taking into account the report to be received from the deputies and also including consideration of boundary questions, questions of the Ruhr and Rhineland, and others;
4. United States draft disarmament and demilitarization treaty and other measures for political, economic, and military control of Germany;
5. Consideration of the report already submitted by the Committee of Coal Experts; and
6. Consideration of the report of the deputies on the Austrian treaty.

The deputies appointed for discussion of German questions, who are now meeting in London, were instructed to: (*a*) hear the views of governments of neighboring Allied states and of other Allied states who participated with their armed forces in the common struggle against Germany and who wish to present their views on the German problem; (*b*) consider questions of procedure with regard to the preparation of a peace treaty for Germany; and (*c*) submit a report on the above matters to the Council of Foreign Ministers by February 25, 1947.

The deputies appointed for Austria were instructed to: (*a*) proceed with the preparation of a treaty recognizing the independence of Austria, taking into consideration the proposals already submitted by the Governments of the United States and the United Kingdom, as well as any further proposals which may be submitted by any member of the Council of Foreign Ministers; (*b*) hear the views of the governments of neighboring Allied states and of other Allied states who participated with their armed forces in the common struggle against Germany and who wish to present their views on the Austrian problem; and (*c*) submit proposals on the above matters to the Council of Foreign Ministers by February 25, 1947.

Thus, in addition to the completion of the five peace treaties which was its primary charge, the Council of Foreign Ministers at its third session in New York made the first real progress in the direction of the consideration of the even more important problems regarding the future of Germany and Austria.

APPENDIX 15

Address by James F. Byrnes, Secretary of State, at the Institute of the Cleveland Council on World Affairs, January 11, 1947

TWICE IN OUR generation the communities of America have learned that they are very much a part of the world when the world is at war. If we are to prevent war and build enduring peace, every community in America must realize that it is very much a part of the world when the world is at peace.

Our first task is to liquidate the war. We cannot think constructively about the building of lasting peace and about rising standards of life until we give the peoples of this world a chance to live again under conditions of peace. We cannot deal with the problems of a convalescing world until we get the patient off the operating table.

That is why President Truman and I at Potsdam two months after V–E Day proposed to set up the Council of Foreign Ministers to start work upon the peace treaties as quickly as possible wherever possible.

That is why we have persistently urged since last winter that deputies should be appointed to begin work upon the German and Austrian treaties.

After every great war the victorious Allies have found it difficult to adjust their differences in the making of peace. At the very outset grave differences between the Allies did arise in the work of the Council of Foreign Ministers. But we refused to abandon the principles for which our country stands. And we served notice that we would not retreat to a policy of isolation.

We made it clear that as anxious as we were to reduce the burden of occupation, America would not evade her responsibility. And we also made it clear that as long as our Allies maintained troops in Germany and Austria, the United States would maintain its troops in those countries.

We were determined to do our part to bring peace to a war-weary world and we have not sought any excuse, however plausible, for shirking our responsibilities.

The treaties with Italy and the ex-satellite states, as they emerged from months of protracted negotiation and debate, are not perfect.

But they are as good as we can hope to get by general agreement now or within a reasonable length of time.

The treaties mark a milestone on the return to conditions of peace. The fact that the Allies have been able to agree upon these five treaties does give hope that they will soon be able to agree upon a treaty with Austria. That will make possible the removal of occupation troops from all European countries except Germany, and will give to millions of people relief from the burdens of occupying armies.

Agreement upon these treaties gives assurance too that the discussions of the German settlement will start under much more favorable conditions than seemed possible until last month.

During the year or more that these treaties were under discussion it was inevitable that the differences between the Allies should be emphasized, and at times exaggerated. On the other hand, during the war some of these differences were minimized and overlooked. But peace cannot be made by ignoring very real and basic differences and by pretending they do not exist.

By recognizing and bringing out into the open our differences and honestly seeking means of reconciling them, we have advanced and not retarded the cause of peace.

The discussions and debates in the Council of Foreign Ministers and in the Security Council during the past year caused a better understanding of our problems and contributed much to the substantial progress made at the recent Assembly of the United Nations.

But we would never have made the progress that we did during the last year if the American people had not been united on a foreign policy.

For the past year our foreign policy has not been the policy of a political party; it has been the policy of the United States.

And I am sure my Democratic friend Senator Connally would join me in saying that our bi-partisan foreign policy was made possible only by the whole-hearted and intelligent cooperation of my Republican friend Senator Arthur Vandenberg.

I would issue a word of caution against excessive optimism and excessive pessimism.

We must not let ourselves believe that peace can be made secure by any one treaty or series of treaties, or by any one resolution or series of resolutions. And we must not let ourselves believe that the struggle for peace is hopeless because we cannot at once find ways and means of reconciling all our differences.

Nations, like individuals, differ as to what is right and just, and clashing appeals to reason may in the long run do more to avert a clash of arms than a lot of pious resolutions which conceal honest and serious disagreements.

Never before have the differences between nations been brought out into the open and so frankly discussed in public as they have during the past year in the Council of Foreign Ministers, the Security Council, and the General Assembly.

Of course it is true that public discussion emphasizes differences. But without such public discussion the people of the world who want peace would not know and understand the differences which arise between nations and which threaten the peace.

Wars may start not because the people want war, but because they want things that other people possess and will not give up without a fight. Full and frank discussion of such situations may avert armed conflict.

The struggle for peace is the struggle for law and justice. It is a never-ending struggle. Law and justice can be developed and applied only through living institutions capable of life and growth. And these institutions must be backed by sufficient force to protect nations which abide by the law against nations which violate the law.

If we are going to build a regime of law among nations, we must struggle to create a world in which no nation can arbitrarily impose its will upon any other nation. Neither the United States nor any other state should have the power to dominate the world.

The present power relationships of the great states preclude the domination of the world by any one of them. Those power relationships cannot be substantially altered by the unilateral action of any one state without profoundly disturbing the whole structure of the United Nations.

Therefore, if we are going to do our part to maintain peace under law, we must maintain in relation to other states, the military strength necessary to discharge our obligations. Force does not make right, but we must realize that in this imperfect world, power as well as reason does affect international decisions.

The great states are given special responsibility under the Charter because they have the military strength to maintain peace if they have the will to maintain peace. Their strength in relation to one another is such that no one of them can safely break the peace if the others stand united in defense of the Charter.

We have joined with our Allies in the United Nations to put an end to war. We have covenanted not to use force except in defense of law. We shall keep that covenant.

As a great power and as a permanent member of the Security Council, we have a responsibility, veto or no veto, to see that other states do not use force except in defense of law. We must discharge that responsibility.

And we must realize that unless the great powers are not only prepared to observe the law but are prepared to act in defense of the law, the United Nations organization cannot prevent war.

In a world in which people do differ as to what is right and wrong, we must strive to work out definite standards of conduct which all can accept. We must develop and build through the years a common law of nations.

History informs us that individuals abandoned private wars and gave up their arms only as they were protected by the common law of their tribe and their nation. So I believe that in the long run international peace depends upon our ability to develop a common law of nations which all nations can accept and which no nation can violate with impunity.

In the past international law has concerned itself too much with the rules of war and too little with the rules of peace. I am more interested in ways and means to prevent war than in ways and means to conduct war.

Unless we are able to develop a common law of nations which provides definite and agreed standards of conduct such as those which govern decisions within the competence of the International Court of Justice and such as those which we hope may be agreed upon for the control of atomic energy, international problems between sovereign states must be worked out by agreement between sovereign states.

The United States has taken the lead in proposing the control and the elimination from national armaments of atomic weapons and other weapons of mass destruction under agreed rules of law.

These rules of law must carry clear and adequate safeguards to protect complying states from the hazards of violations and evasions. They must be sufficiently definite and explicit to prevent a state that violates the law from obstructing the prompt and effective enforcement of the law.

If a nation by solemn treaty agrees to a plan for the control of atomic weapons and agrees that a violation of that treaty shall be punished, it is difficult for me to understand why that nation cannot agree to waive the right to exercise the veto power should it be charged with violating its treaty obligation.

In 1921 while a member of the House I advocated that the President call a conference for the limitation of naval armaments.

Later the President did call such a conference. What happened thereafter influences my thinking today. While America scrapped battleships, Japan scrapped blueprints.   America will not again make that mistake.

We have urged a general limitation of armaments, but we are not going to disarm while others remain armed.   And we should make certain that all governments live up to their agreements to disarm.

We have urged priority for the control of atomic weapons because they are the most destructive of all weapons, because we have been at work on the proposal for more than six months, and because it presents concretely the issue of international inspection and control. We are convinced that if there can be agreement on that subject, there can be agreement on the control of other major weapons and a general reduction of armaments.

But international law in a friendly, peaceful world must rest upon something more than mere rules, something more than force, and something more than fear.   It must be made to rest upon the growth of a common fellowship, common interests, and common ideas among the peoples of this earth.

It was our fostering of a common fellowship that gave vitality to the good-neighbor policy in the Americas.   It was a common fellowship which made the Act of Chapultepec possible.

We are eager to proceed with a negotiation of a mutual-assistance treaty in accordance with the Act of Chapultepec at the projected Rio de Janeiro conference.   But we do not wish to proceed without Argentina and neither our Ambassador nor any official of the State Department is of the opinion that Argentina has yet complied with the commitments which she as well as the other American republics at Chapultepec agreed to carry out.

It is our earnest hope that before long there will be such reasonable and substantial compliance by Argentina with its obligations, that the American republics after consultation will convene the Rio conference.

A common fellowship does not mean that nations must in all respects think alike or live alike.   Inevitably we will differ.   But nations like individuals must respect and tolerate one another's differences.

Peace in this interdependent world must be something more than a truce between nations.   To have peace, nations must learn to live and work together for their common good.   We live in one world.   The health of the body politic like the health of the human body depends upon the health of all its members.

We cannot whole-heartedly abandon the policy of political isolation unless we abandon the policy of economic isolation.   We are not likely to be successful in our efforts to cooperate to prevent war, unless we are willing to cooperate to maintain freedom and well-being in a world at peace.

We must learn to cooperate so that the people of each country may exchange the products of their country easily and fairly with the people of other countries.

Although our general long-run purpose is to help raise the living standard, the immediate problem during the last two years in some areas has been to maintain life itself.

Economic distress, starvation, and disease breed political unrest, tyranny, and aggression. If we are sincere in our efforts to maintain peace, we must do our part to assist in the elimination of conditions which breed aggression and war.

If we want people to value freedom and respect law we must at least give them a fair chance to feed, clothe, and shelter themselves and their families.

The war has devastated many countries and disrupted their economies. UNRRA has helped these countries through their most critical period. Its authority is terminated but some countries through no fault of their own will require further relief to get upon their feet. And this we must not deny them.

Outright relief by us is necessary in some countries. But the countries in need and the extent of the need can be determined by the United States just as well as it could be determined by a committee composed of representatives of other governments.

A permanent place on the relief rolls is not the desire of those self-respecting nations which have fought for their freedom. But much of their productive capacity has been destroyed, and they have no working capital in the form of foreign exchange to start the flow of needed raw materials.

They do need loans to secure the raw materials, capital, equipment, and tools necessary to rebuild and resume their ability to produce. The work of the International Bank, the International Monetary Fund, and our own Export-Import Bank must continue to have our whole-hearted support.

Despite the ravages and destruction of the war, the advances of science make it possible for us and other nations to preserve and increase our living standards if we work together with other nations to produce what we and other nations want and need.

We must learn that prosperity like freedom must be shared, not on the basis of hand-outs, but on the basis of fair and honest exchange of the products of the labor of free men and free women.

We believe that there should be no unnecessary barriers to the free exchange of ideas and information among nations. But it is unreal-

istic to expect to have trade in ideas if we are unwilling to have trade in goods.

We must do our part to break down the artificial barriers to trade and commerce among nations. We must pursue vigorously our reciprocal trade policies which are designed to expand American trade and world trade because the world cannot buy from us if we are not willing to buy from the world.

We must pursue vigorously our proposed charter for the establishment of an International Trade Organization. That charter is designed to avoid economic warfare between nations and to insure equality of commercial opportunity for all nations, both large and small. We must avoid economic blocs if we wish to avoid political blocs.

After every great war there comes a period of disillusionment. Those who fight together expect too much from one another and are inclined to give too little to one another. They forget that victory in war can only give the opportunity which would otherwise be denied, to live and work for the fruits of peace and freedom.

I admit that during the past year there were times when I was deeply discouraged. Our repeated efforts to achieve cooperation in a peaceful world seemed to be meeting only with constant rebuff. But we persisted in our efforts with patience and with firmness.

Today I am happy to say that I am more confident than at any time since V–J Day that we can achieve a just peace by cooperative effort if we persist "with firmness in the right as God gives us the power to see the right."

We have demonstrated our capacity in war. We must demonstrate our capacity in peace. If we do, our children and the children of men everywhere can inherit a peaceful world of expanding freedom and increased well-being.

To that goal freedom's past inspires us and freedom's future calls us.

O